Rescue Matters!

Dedication

To Reno, the embodiment of courage, beauty, forgiveness, and love.
You are my doggy hero.

Other books by Sheila Webster Boneham:

The Multiple Dog Family (T.F.H. Publications, 2009)

Shetland Sheepdogs (T.F.H. Publications, 2009)

Training Your Dog for Life (T.F.H. Publications, 2008)

The Multiple Cat Family (T.F.H. Publications, 2008)

Senior Cats (T.F.H. Publications, 2008) – Award of Excellence, Cat Writers Association

Dachshunds (T.F.H. Publications, 2007)

Parson and Jack Russell Terriers (T.F.H. Publications, 2006)

Golden Retrievers (T.F.H. Publications, 2006)

The Complete Idiot's Guide to Getting and Owning a Cat (Alpha Books, 2005) – MUSE Award
    for Best Care and Health Book, and Award of Excellence, Cat Writers Association

The Boxer (T.F.H. Publications, 2005)

The Simple Guide to the Labrador Retriever (T.F.H. Publications, 2003) – Maxwell Award,
    Best Single Breed Book, Dog Writers Association of America

The Complete Idiot's Guide to Getting and Owning a Dog (Alpha Books, 2001) – Maxwell
    Award, Best General Reference Book, Dog Writers Association of America

The Owner's Guide to the Australian Shepherd (T.F.H. Publications, 2000)

The Owner's Guide to the Pembroke Welsh Corgi (T.F.H. Publications, 2000)

Breed Rescue: How to Start and Run a Successful Program (Alpine, 1998) – Maxwell Award,
    Best General Reference Book, Dog Writers Association of America

Rescue Matters!

How to Find, Foster, and Rehome Companion Animals

A GUIDE FOR VOLUNTEERS AND ORGANIZERS

Sheila Webster Boneham, Ph.D.

Crawford, Colorado

RESCUE MATTERS:
How to Find, Foster, and Rehome Companion Animals:
A Guide for Volunteers and Organizers

ISBN 13: 978-1-57779-101-0
ISBN 10: 1-57779-101-0

Library of Congress Cataloging-in-Publication Data

Boneham, Sheila Webster, 1952-
Rescue matters : how to find, foster, and rehome companion animals : a guide
for volunteers and organizers / by Sheila Webster Boneham.
        p. cm.
    Includes bibliographical references and index.
    ISBN-13: 978-1-57779-101-0 (pbk. : alk. paper)
    ISBN-10: 1-57779-101-0 (pbk. : alk. paper)
    1. Animal rescue—United States. 2. Animal welfare—United States. 3. Pets.
    I. Title.

    HV4735.B67 2009
    636.08′320973—dc22   2008045383

The information contained in this book is complete and accurate to the best of our knowledge. All recommendations are made without guarantee on the part of the author or Alpine Publications, Inc. The author and publisher disclaim any liability with the use of this information. Readers are advised to consult with a professional regarding all medical or legal advice herein.

This book is available at special quantity discounts for breeders and rescuers and for club promotions, premiums, or educational use. Write for details.

For the sake of simplicity, the terms " he" or "she" are sometimes used to identify an animal or person. These are used in the generic sense only. No discrimination of any kind is intended toward either sex.

Many manufacturers secure trademark rights for their products. When Alpine Publications is aware of a trademark claim, we identify the product name by using initial capital letters.

Cover Design: Kelly Keller, Grafik Nature
Editing: Sheila Dolan
Layout: Dianne Nelson
Photographs by the author unless otherwise indicated.

Printed in the United States of America.

TABLE OF CONTENTS

FOREWORD

I speak now only of dogs, for I am so allergic to cats that I have no experience of them, nor have I been so drawn to other species as I have been drawn to dogs.

No matter how rewarding it may be, any relationship between two human beings —between parent and child, between siblings, between spouses—will have its problems, its strained moments, because we are fallen, because each of us has faults, because even the best of us are to some degree self-centered. A relationship with a good dog, however, can approach perfection, because dogs are innocent, because they are willing to be trained out of what bad habits they may have, and because their love is pure. As Josh Billings famously said, "A dog is the only thing on Earth that loves you more than he loves himself."

In file, I have hundreds of stories about dogs risking their lives – and sometimes losing them – for the human members of their families. No other species on the planet will make the ultimate sacrifice for us. In A.D. 79, Pompeii was buried in volcanic ash. Centuries later, excavators discovered a dog lying across a child, trying to protect it from the eruption. According to an inscription on his collar, the dog, Delta, had previously saved the life of his owner three times.

Frankly, many human beings are not worthy of the unconditional love and the total commitment that dogs make to them. Every day, these animals are abused, neglected, abandoned. The breeding dogs in puppy mills spend their entire lives suffering in cramped cages, brutalized, terrorized, malnourished and denied all affection, in order that the monsters who own these enterprises and the pet stores they sell to can satisfy their greed.

God continues to allow the existence of humanity perhaps in part because there are good people who step forward to rescue the dogs that have been abandoned or cruelly mistreated. Every person I have ever met in dog rescue programs has proved to be committed, caring and ethical. Good people, of course, are drawn to good causes; but I also believe that when people are moved by the plight of these animals and open their hearts to them, they become better people because of the experience. Dogs can transform us; if we will let them, they can be our redeemers.

Sheila Boneham, long involved in animal rescue, has written this book to show caring people how to organize against this cruelty and disturbing indifference, and how to apply their compassion and their energy to the salvation of these beautiful creatures. We and our companion animals are souls in transit from one life to another. Every dog I've ever known is aware of this. And those human beings who open their hearts to this truth and who extend their loving hands to animals in need have surely earned for themselves the tender consideration of Heaven.

Dean Koontz, 2008

PREFACE

Women, I believe, have a special relationship with animals of all kinds. Most rescue volunteers are women. More women than men compete in animal-based sports, and many serious, responsible breeders are women. Female veterinarians and vet students now outnumber their male colleagues, and the membership rosters of the Dog Writers Association of America and the Cat Writers Association are predominantly female. I am not suggesting that the work of men on behalf of animals is less valuable or less appreciated, or their love of animals less profound, but to better reflect reality I use the "generic feminine" in this book to refer to rescue volunteers, breeders, and veterinarians. For contrast and clarity, I use masculine pronouns for animals and their owners, although of course rescued animals come in both sexes, as do the people who affect their lives.

Much of the information in this book appeared in an earlier form in *Breed Rescue: How to Start and Run a Successful Program* (Alpine, 1997), in which I focused on the rescue of purebred dogs. This book, in contrast, addresses issues that affect rescuers of all household companion animals, and much of the discussion extends to other domestic animals as well as exotic animals that people keep as pets.

If you are new to rescue work, or you are thinking of becoming involved, I hope the information and ideas expressed here will help you make informed and thoughtful choices at the start of your journey. If you have been on this path for a while, I hope the book will help you negotiate some of the inevitable obstacles and remind you that, rough as it is, the rescue road is strewn with blossoms that make it worth the walk. I hope I have succeeded.

Sheila Webster Boneham, Ph.D.
January 2009

ACKNOWLEDGMENTS

I grew up in a "rescue home." Animals–dogs, cats, horses, several parakeets, a couple of hamsters, a bunch of chinchillas, and an injured bob-white–were part of the family. (I never did get the Jersey heifer I wanted!) Strays arrived on our doorstep with some regularity to be cared for and then returned to their owners, or placed in new homes, or–more than once–to stay.

Both my parents loved and respected animals, my mother in particular. I was nurtured on stories of the animals in her life, and have always felt a kinship to the cats, dogs, horses, hen, magpie, and rat of whom she spoke often and fondly, all gone long before I was born but living still in my storied memory. For that legacy I am grateful.

My husband has been my rock (he is, after all, a geologist) for almost two decades. Thanks, Roger, for welcoming, loving, and caring for all the animals, and me. Wait 'til you see what I bring home next!

A book cannot be born without the labors of many people. I can't possibly identify everyone who has supported my efforts as a writer, but I must point to a few. Lisa A. Notestine, DVM, MT (ASCP), read the draft of Chapter 8 and kept me as honest as she could about veterinary issues. Jody Young, Former Assistant National Director of Ridgeback Rescue of the US, Inc., and Peggy Mundell, President of San Diego Spaniel Rescue, provided ideas and information for this book and cheered me on. I also especially appreciate the kindness and encouragement I've received from Dorothy Christianson, national coordinator of Shetland Sheepdog Rescue; mystery writer extraordinaire Susan Conant; and Sharyn and Walter Hutchens, who for many years have taken on the task of monitoring the BreedRescue discussion list, which is mine in name but theirs in many ways. The members of that list have also been a tremendous resource for me and, I think, for one another. Betty McKinney of Alpine Publications had faith in my first book years ago, and has supported this expanded approach to the literature of rescue. Her assistant, Tammy Hayes, is a fountain of information and ideas to light the author's path. My profound thanks to all of you. All opinions, omissions, and goofs in the book are, of course, my own.

Finally, first, and above all, my love, respect, and gratitude to the fauna of the world, especially those who have agreed to live with us humans despite our many faults, and to enrich our lives and souls.

INTRODUCTION

We know from archeological evidence that dogs and cats wove themselves into people's lives and hearts at least ten thousand years ago, living in human dwellings, inspiring human art, sharing human work, and being buried in or near human graves. Other creatures were not far behind.

I suspect that compassion played a part in some of these early interactions, perhaps the adoption of an orphaned baby animal, or the rescue and nursing of a sick or injured creature. If such events occurred, then things haven't changed all that much because people are still rescuing animals from pain, abuse, and loneliness. Some rescue efforts are unplanned acts of kindness brought on by circumstance. Others result from people's ongoing commitment to seek out and help animals that are in trouble, and to bring them together with people who will respect and care for them. The world of organized pet rescue has grown exponentially in the past two decades, and now involves many thousands of people working to make life better for all kinds of animals, from "pocket pets" like hamster and gerbils, to "conventional" pets like dogs and cats, to reptiles, birds, exotic animals, and large animals.

Rescue programs offer certain advantages over community shelters. Volunteers in breed- or species-specific rescue programs are "specialists" and thus often better able than the average shelter worker to assess an individual animal's behavior, training needs, and suitability for placement. They are (or should be) well informed about the potential for specific genetic problems, and know what to look for to increase the chances that adopters will get healthy pets, or know in advance about problems. They can give accurate advice about the animal's exercise, nutritional, grooming, and housing requirements. Shelter workers, no matter how dedicated and knowledgeable, cannot be experts on every kind of animal they handle. Breed- or species-specific rescuers, on the other hand, are in an excellent position to make informed matches between pets and people.

The rescue program also has a clear advantage over individual efforts, for this is an area where there truly is strength in numbers. Rescue is not all glamour and happy endings. It involves long hours, hard physical and mental work, diplomacy, disappointment, heartache, and risk. People who band together to face the difficulties—and share the joys—accomplish more and last longer than do solitary rescuers.

Although most breeds of dogs and cats, as well as certain other animals, have national rescue organizations, the work of rescue is almost always done at the local level, and many rescuers prefer to band together in autonomous local groups. Whether you hope to organize a new group, enhance an existing one, volunteer with a rescue organization, or rescue animals on your own, I hope that *Rescue Matters!* has something for you.

PART

1

People and Policies

CHAPTER

1

Getting Organized

We all know people who have taken in and rehomed the occasional stray animal. You're probably one of them, and if you plan to rescue only whenever an animal in need finds you—the best time to do it!—then you can skip this chapter. But if you want to escalate your efforts, there are good reasons to unite with other like-minded people. Why?

For one thing, although rescue work is rewarding, it can also be time consuming, emotionally and physically exhausting, expensive, and potentially hazardous. Placing a live animal in a new home carries risks. Adopters vary wildly in their knowledge of animals, their life-styles, their willingness to follow suggestions from rescuers, and their tolerance of normal "life with pets." If you rescue animals on a regular basis, you incur legal and financial liability. All in all, a group effort is more efficient, usually longer lived, and safer.

If you are a rescue-group organizer, formal structure will support your work and your volunteers in many ways, and give you credibility as a serious entity devoted to the welfare of both animals and people. If you volunteer in the trenches of animal rescue, a structured community will comfort and support you when the work is sad or hard, and will bring the pleasures of shared celebration when rescue goes right.

HOW TO ORGANIZE

The mundane work of organizing may seem to be a waste of the time you'd like to devote directly to animals in need, but in the long run you'll be glad you did it. To organize for effective rescue work, you need to:

- Set up a governing body.
- Establish points of contact.
- Incorporate.
- Establish policies and procedures.
- Write legal documents.
- Obtain insurance.

WHO'S IN CHARGE HERE?

A group without leadership is prone to chaos, no matter how well meaning, hard working, and like-minded the individual members are. Even if your group is small, designating clear responsibilities for each person will increase efficiency and let you accomplish more with less effort. As membership in your group increases, organization becomes essential.

One of the first steps is to set up a governing body. If your group is part of a larger organization, such as a breed club, officers of the rescue program may be determined by the larger group. If you are independent, or if the umbrella organization prefers to grant you more autonomy, you will select a governing body from among yourselves.

Typically, rescue groups elect a board of directors (BOD) composed of officers (president, vice president, treasurer, and secretary) and directors (*see* "Incorporation"). Many groups also elect or appoint a Volunteer Coordinator to screen and assign volunteers (*see* Chapter 3), an Adoption Coordinator to oversee placements (Chapter 10), and a Foster Coordinator to oversee assessment of incoming animals and to assign them to specific foster homes (Chapters 6, 8, and 9). As your group expands, you may need to establish and fill additional jobs.

The officers and directors should be chosen carefully, as they will determine many of the group's policies and practices, and will be the "face" of the group to shelters, other rescue groups, breeders, fanciers, and the general public. Enthusiasm for saving animals, although essential, is not enough for effective leadership. Anyone who represents your group to other people must also be well informed, diplomatic, reliable, and articulate. (*See* Chapter 3 on screening volunteers, and apply the same principles doubled to the governing body.)

Marley was one of my first Lab rescues, and one of my all-time favorites. At eleven years of age, he was relinquished to Labrador Retriever Rescue of Indiana, Inc., by people who had owned him since he was six weeks old. When I picked him up, he was in a filthy pen at a relative's farm, and had already been replaced by a new puppy. This lovely, gentle dog spent the day being checked by our vet and bathed, and met his new family the same evening. He spent the rest of his life with the Irwins of Indianapolis, taking daily walks and frequent swims in a nearby park, loving and being loved. PHOTO BY SHEILA BONEHAM.

WHERE ARE YOU? POINTS OF CONTACT

Your rescue group must be accessible to potential donors, adopters, and volunteers, and, of course, people with animals they want or need to place. Although some rescuers use their personal contact information for their rescue work, it's not always a good idea. The majority of people who contact rescue are reasonable and rational. Some, though, act as if rescuers should be at their beck and call 24/7, and a few are nutty enough that you might not want them to call your home phone or know where you live.

In fairness, people don't always realize that rescue groups are composed of volunteers who shouldn't have to take calls when they're in the middle of something else, pooped, or just not in a position or frame of mind to give or take information. Besides, rescue calls day and night aren't fair to the rest of your human household, no matter how sympathetic and supportive they are. Using your home phone and address also creates a problem when you leave town, whether for a day or a week, or when you need someone else to take over the communication duties for a while, and the results of giving out your personal cell number may drive you completely bonkers.

Fortunately, the explosion of new communication media over the past decade works to the advantage of new-millennium rescuers. Ideally, your group will utilize several of the following options.

E-mail
You need one or more e-mail addresses dedicated to rescue. Include an e-mail address on the group web site (*see below*) and on all printed material. Several servers offer free e-mail accounts, and most web-site hosting services include one or more e-mail accounts as part of the web site. You can give access to the account to any volunteer who has Internet service, and you can restrict access by means of a password, which can be changed if necessary.

Be careful about who has access to and responsibility for group-owned addresses. Nothing deflects interest so quickly as a rude or uninformative response, or no response at all. Here are some tips for making e-mail work for your group:

- Reply to all e-mails within 72 hours, and set up an automatic response to go out immediately to let people know that a volunteer will reply soon.
- Be sure that whoever replies to e-mails is reliable, prompt, knowledgeable, and civil.
- Rotate e-mail duties to avoid volunteer burn out (or assign one volunteer to e-mail duty only). The higher the volume of incoming e-mail, the more often you should change responders.
- Create standard replies for FAQs (Frequently Asked Questions). Refer people to these FAQs on your web site, or paste them into e-mail replies.
- If people have questions or concerns not covered by your FAQs, reply to those individually.
- Keep copies of important e-mails for at least several months, and file them by subject, sender, and/or date so you can find them if you need them.

Web Site
Web sites have become *de rigueur* for any serious entity. A good web site provides many benefits. It's an excellent way to educate people and to thank your adopters, volunteers, donors, and supporters. It also gives you the perfect way to spotlight animals you have up for adoption, and those you have placed in homes.

You don't need a computer geek to set up your site. I have nothing against professional web design, but the fact is that you don't need to know an arcane computer language or complicated program, and you don't need to spend a fortune to put up an attractive, functional site. Several companies offer "WYSIWYG" (What You See Is What You Get) web design programs that guide anyone with reasonable computer competence through the process (one good one is homestead.com).

Some companies offer free web sites. They work well for many rescue groups, but before you leap into a free site, check the terms of service. "Free" web hosts make their money by selling advertising that appears on the web sites they host. You cannot control the advertising that appears on your site, and I've seen some pretty shady pet-business links pop up on rescue group sites. The fine print for a few servers also gives them the right to copy and use or sell anything you put on your free web site.

The cost of paid web-site hosting varies depending on the company and the options you choose, and could run a couple hundred dollars a year. But if you have the resources, that may be money well spent, because you control what appears on your site. Some companies offer special rates for not-for-profit organizations. Many rescue groups also defray the cost of their web sites by becoming affiliates of various commercial sites that are compatible with their philosophies and goals. If you publish a "Wish List" (*see* Chapter 4), put "Web Sponsorships" on the list and perhaps you can get one or more people or companies to donate money earmarked for your web site. You might also be able to set up as a free subsidiary site on someone else's web site, with your own url, if their server offers that option.

Be sure to set up metatags (codes that enable search engines to find your site when people search with certain terms)—most web-site servers will show you how. Promote your site to search engines so that it will appear early in search results for a range of relevant terms, and contact the webmasters at other appropriate web sites to set up reciprocal links.

Telephone

A lot of rescue work is done over the phone. If your group is one of the few that have a fixed physical location, you'll no doubt set up a "business" phone line. Most rescue groups don't have a central "headquarters," though, and although volunteers' home and mobile phones serve well for communication within the group, you need at least one official phone number. Here are some ideas for setting up a viable rescue phone system.

- Voice Mail: A line answered only by voice mail works just fine, as long as you return calls in a timely manner. Voice mail boxes protect the privacy of volunteers' home numbers, make it easy to rotate phone duty, shield other household members from incoming rescue calls, and enable volunteers to return calls at their convenience, when they are prepared for rescue-related conversations. They also prevent dead numbers when volunteers move. All you need is a dedicated telephone number and a message box that can be accessed with a code. Many telephone companies offer voice-mail services for less per month than secretarial companies, but shop around, and ask about special rates for not-for-profit groups.

- Cell Phones: A dedicated cell phone account works well for some groups, and pre-paid cell phones don't require long-term contracts. Like voice-mail boxes, cell phones can be passed from one volunteer to another, calls can be sent to voice mail when the volunteer is not available, and most cell phone companies offer free long distance at certain times. Choose only those features that your work requires, and be sure that incoming calls are free.
- Toll-Free Numbers: If your group covers a large geographic area, a toll-free number for incoming calls may be a good option. These so-called "800 numbers" are available through different companies, so compare features, cost, and commitment before you sign up.

How to Set Up User-friendly Voice Mail

Nothing is more frustrating to a caller than a voice-mail system that doesn't work properly. Here are some tips to make yours work:

- Write and tweak your message, and then have a volunteer with a good speaking voice record it. Check that the recording is clear and good quality.
- Identify your group and make it clear that the caller has reached a voice-mail system staffed by volunteers, and that he must leave a number in order to speak to someone.
- Specify a time frame in which calls will be returned. Don't promise a return call within 24 hours if 72 hours is more realistic. It's better to return the call sooner than people expect rather than later.
- Refer callers to your web site, if you have one.
- If you don't have access to free long distance, specify that calls may be returned collect.
- Remind callers to leave a name, number, and good time to call, and to briefly explain what kind of information they need.

Postal Address

Despite the e-mail revolution, your group still needs a postal address. For one thing, you must have an address if you want to incorporate (later in this chapter). You also need an address to receive applications, donations, and other material by mail.

You could use an individual volunteer's address, but that's not the best idea for several reasons. First, it's important to preserve the privacy of volunteers, which includes the location of their homes. Second, if that volunteer moves or leaves the group, or if someone else takes over mail duty, you'll have to change your mailing address on all your material, and you may lose some mail.

Post offices and private companies offer mailboxes at reasonable rates, and some have lower rates for not-for-profit groups. For convenience, look for a service with around-the-clock mailbox access or a mail-forwarding service that receives the mail and then sends it on to a designated address. Mail forwarding allows for changes in mail duties without requiring a change of mailing address or long drives for volunteers.

INCORPORATION

Rescue activities can carry legal and financial liability. As an active rescuer, you may be perceived legally as an expert, and may therefore be held responsible in a court of law for decisions or recommendations you make. If you are an officer or board member of a rescue group, your responsibility may extend not only to adopters and prior owners of animals you take in, but also to volunteers. Legal liability for a bad decision (or a reasonable decision that works out badly) could put not just your shirt but your house, bank accounts, and other assets at risk.

The best way to protect members of your group from personal liability is to incorporate, which shifts liability from individual rescuers to the corporation. If your group qualifies under federal regulations, incorporation as a 501c not-for-profit organization makes donations to your group tax deductible for the donors and may relieve your group of the obligation to pay state sales tax. (*See also* Chapter 4.)

How to Incorporate as a Not-for-Profit Organization

To acquire federal not-for-profit status as a 501c corporation, you must file Form 1023 with the United States Internal Revenue Service (IRS) within fifteen months from the date you incorporate under state law. Try to borrow and adapt from a rescue group that has already qualified as a 501c corporation, because the IRS agent reviewing the application may want to see certain language in the articles or bylaws. Getting it right the first time will speed up the process.

Consult an attorney to ensure that your group chooses the most appropriate form of legal organization and completes all requirements in a proper and timely fashion. Many law firms and individual attorneys offer *pro bono* (free) legal services under certain conditions, but even if you have to pay, professional legal advice is worth the investment.

Although state laws differ, incorporation typically requires applicants to take the following steps:

- Establish a governing board of directors and elect or appoint officers.
- Draft a mission statement.
- Adopt Articles of Incorporation and Bylaws.

Legal Corporation or Alter Ego?

Organization as a corporation or other form of legal entity can limit your members' personal liability. It's essential, though, that you organize properly so that a court will not rule that the corporation is an *alter ego,* or front, for an individual, who could then be held personally liable for damages in a law suit. Consult an attorney to be sure you are in compliance with state laws.

Leo was brought to my veterinarian after wandering around an apartment complex for a week or so. He had a penchant for shredding upholstery, which may be why he was dumped. Dr. Charles McCune examined and vaccinated him, and fostered him, as he has done for many animals in need. When my husband and I were in the clinic a few days later, Priscilla McCune, Dr. McCune's wife and assistant, told Roger he needed to see something in the back room. It was love at first sight; Leo came home with us, and fit right in with the rest of the cats and dogs. PHOTO BY SHEILA BONEHAM.

The Mission Statement

Your *mission statement* describes the purpose, or mission, of your organization. A good rescue mission statement identifies the group and the types of animal(s) covered by the group's activities, and states why these activities are important.

Sample Mission Statement

The mission of Labrador Retriever Rescue of Indiana, Inc. is to take in purebred Labrador Retrievers that are in shelters, whose owners no longer want them, or that have become lost and abandoned, and to place them in permanent pet homes in order to help provide a safe harbor for Labrador Retrievers that might otherwise be destroyed.

Articles of Incorporation and Bylaws

A group's *Articles of Incorporation* identify the incorporators and set forth the purpose of the organization. The *Bylaws* state how officers will be selected, how often meetings will be held, how and when elections will be held, and other organizational and management details. Articles of incorporation and bylaws are fairly standard, and you may be able to adapt a set from another rescue group or other not-for-profit organization to meet your state's legal requirements.

ESTABLISHING POLICIES AND PROCEDURES

Standard policies and procedures are always a good idea, and they become critical as your group takes on more personnel. They promote consistency in what your volunteers say and do on behalf of the group, and may save you considerable trouble by taking certain decisions out of the individuals' hands. The process of setting policies and standard operating procedures also helps people think through many potential issues before they crop up. If you are new to rescue work, talk to experienced rescuers or join an e-mail group or two to get an idea of the sorts of issues that can arise.

If you rescue enough animals and work with enough people, sooner or later you'll encounter a situation that is anything but straightforward. You may hear rescuers say that "you can't save them all," but the emotional reality of that statement won't hit home until you encounter the animal that *you* can't save. Similarly, at some point you'll meet the potential adopter who doesn't fit your usual guidelines, but who seems to be a good candidate nevertheless. Anticipating such situations, and setting policies and procedures to manage them when they occur, can save you time, conflict, and stress.

Well-thought-out written policies and procedures are your *position statement* on responsible pet ownership and other issues, and they position your group on the animal-welfare political continuum. They show that your group is sincere, legitimate, and competent, which can help you establish and maintain good working relationships with animal shelters, other rescue groups, veterinarians, breeders, and donors. For your volunteers, written policies and procedures offer a guide to action and a solid set of answers to people's questions and concerns. They can also help attract potential volunteers and donors.

Sit down with your fellow rescuers and brainstorm predictable problems that could arise as you acquire, assess, foster, and rehome rescued pets. Consult other experienced rescuers, and don't discount the information and ideas you can get from responsible breeders—they often have a wealth of experience and knowledge that can help you assess animals, would-be adopters, and unusual situations.

Policy and procedural decisions usually hinge on several factors, including the financial and human resources available to the group, the number of animals you handle, the length of time that most animals spend in your foster homes, the availability of adopters, and, of course, the type of animal you rescue.

Here are some of the issues to consider as you establish policies and procedures. Some of these apply to any type of pet, while others are species specific. This is not an exhaustive list, but it should get you thinking.

Issues concerning the animals:

- Will you accept mixed-breed animals, or only (apparently) purebred animals?
- How will you ensure that every new animal is screened for contagious diseases or parasites?
- How will you assess each animal's health and temperament?
- Will you pay to acquire animals for rescue? Will you buy them from owners or producers? Pay shelter fees?
- Will you accept seriously ill or injured animals? How far will you go to save their lives? (How will expending resources to save one extraordinarily needy animal affect your ability to help others?)
- Will you foster all animals in your program?
- Will you refer potential adopters to owners who want to rehome their pets?
- Will you refer people to responsible breeders if that seems appropriate?
- Will you try to help people keep their pets if that seems appropriate?
- Will you take in elderly animals, or animals with special needs?
- How will you rehabilitate animals with behavior problems other than aggression?
- Will you accept animals with a history of aggression toward people and/or other animals? Will you place those animals in new homes? If so, how will you assess the animals and potential homes?

- Under what circumstances will you have an animal euthanized? Who will be responsible for making the decision to euthanize, and for taking the animal to the vet or shelter for euthanasia?
- If you take in a pregnant female, will you have her spayed immediately, or foster her through the pregnancy and raise and place her babies? If the latter, how will you arrange for proper pre- and post-natal care for both mother and offspring to promote their physical and emotional health?
- Will you require all animals to be altered (spayed or neutered) prior to placement, or within a specified time limit after placement?
- Will you attempt to contact the animal's breeder, or the rescue or shelter from which the animal was last adopted? Will you release the animal to that breeder, shelter, or rescue group if they so request?
- If the animal comes with registration papers, will you transfer them to the adopter? Will you notify the registry that the animal is in rescue?
- If the original owner of a lost pet surfaces after you have rehomed the animal, will you notify the adopter? (You no longer own the animal and can't return her to the previous owner even if you want to, and you cannot be forced to say where the animal is. But what if it were *your* missing pet? That is the question that should inform your policy.)

Issues concerning adopters:

- How will you collect and verify information about potential adopters?
- How will you notify applicants whom you turn down?
- What specific living conditions will you require adopters to provide for animals they adopt from you? (Visible fencing, indoor/outdoor or strictly indoor environment, training, and so on.)
- What if the adoption doesn't work out, or the adopter becomes unable to care for the animal?
- Will you adopt animals to homes within only a certain area, or farther afield?
- Will you adopt to homes with other pets, or only certain kinds of other pets?
- Will you adopt to homes with young children?
- Will you adopt animals to elderly people or people with serious health issues? If so, will you have provisions for reacquiring the animal should the adopter die or become unable to care for the animal?
- How will you protect the privacy of adopters and people relinquishing animals?
- What, if any, rights will relinquishing owners retain after handing the animal over to you?
- What if an owner wants the animal back after relinquishing him or her to rescue?
- What if an owner finds out that you have his or her lost pet? What if that owner is a breeder, responsible or not, and wants the animal back intact?

Issues concerning volunteers:

- How will you screen volunteers and assign them jobs?
- If a volunteer does not work out, how will you decide to "fire" her, and how will she be notified?

As you establish your policies, keep them reasonable and pay attention to how you word them. It is reasonable to require that adopted animals receive regular veterinary care as recommended by a veterinarian, and that they be housed indoors as companions. It is not reasonable to require annual vaccinations or a specific food. If you trust an adopter enough to hand an animal over to him, you must believe that he will take responsible care of that animal. It's one thing to point people to the information necessary to make informed decisions, but quite another to dictate details of pet care and interfere with the owner's right to decide for his pet.

Euthanasia

Euthanasia is potentially one of the most divisive issues a rescue group can face, and having a policy on euthanasia in place before the need arises will minimize conflict within your group. A carefully considered policy won't make individual decisions easy, but it will help you and your fellow rescuers see past raw emotion to the big picture. Discuss your policy on euthanasia with every potential volunteer before they become active with the group. I also recommend a related policy that specifies who (officers, board members, foster caretakers, other volunteers) may be required to take an animal to be euthanized. This will prevent any one person from having to make all these sad trips. (If someone is reluctant because she has never witnessed humane euthanasia, suggest that she arrange to be present for the euthanasia of an animal whose owner will not be there.) Assisting an animal to such a gentle end is far better than letting him suffer from excessive pain or fear, or letting him injure a person or other animal. It is a tearful act, but an act of love and courage.

Policies can be waived when appropriate, as long as you include a method for doing so in your operating procedures. A waiver might require a majority vote by the governing board, for example, or an executive decision by an officer empowered to override normal policies.

If you do relax or waive a policy, say the "fenced yard" requirement for someone adopting a dog, follow your group's rules for waivers to the letter and document your decision-making process. That way you are protected if, say, Mr. "My Last Three Dogs Ran Away from My Unfenced Yard" complains (or sues) because you turned him down, but you let Mr. Goodowner adopt without any kind of fence. Your records would include both parties' adoption applications, a record of the waiver procedure, and the reason. ("We normally require a fence to ensure both the safety of the adopted dog and adherence by that dog to local and state leash laws, which prohibit dogs from running at large. Based on Mr. Goodowner's history as a responsible dog owner, we are confident that he will keep his dog properly confined even without a fence.") This may sound a little obsessive, but if you waive requirements willy-nilly, your informality may come back to haunt you when someone presses the "why him and not me" issue. "Because we said so" will *not* be considered a good reason in a court of law.

LEGAL DOCUMENTS

It would be hard to overstate the importance of legally worded documents. Your documents do not need to be complicated or written in "legalese," but they do need to be legally binding or they are virtually worthless should a violation take you to court. The best way to ensure that your documents are enforceable is to have an attorney examine them *before* you use them.

You don't want to turn your rescue program into a baby bureaucracy that generates mounds of paperwork. On the other hand, legal paperwork is essential to protect the animals you work to save, and to protect your group, your volunteers, and your adopters. Some documents that many rescue groups have found useful include the following:

- *Release of Ownership* form by which legal ownership or possession of an animal is released by an individual to your organization. The last thing you need is to be accused of stealing someone's pet, or euthanizing an animal that the owner believed would be placed in a new home.
- *Release of Ownership or Custody* form by which ownership or possession of an animal is released to your group by a shelter, pound, or other rescue organization. (*See* "Animals from Shelters and Other Rescue Programs" in Chapter 6.)
- *Foster Care* agreements specifying the rights and responsibilities of your foster caretakers with regard to the animals in their care. (*See* Chapters 2 and 3.)
- *Volunteer Agreements* specifying what volunteers may and may not do as representatives of your organization. (*See* Chapters 2 and 3.)
- *Adoption* contracts written to protect the animals, the rescue program and its volunteers, and the adopter. (*See* Chapter 10.)

INSURANCE

Insurance can be expensive, but the cost of having no insurance can be devastating. In the litigious world in which we live, liability insurance is particularly important.

Other types of insurance may also be advisable for your group, depending on how you are organized legally, what assets you possess, what activities you engage in, and what kind of animals you rescue. Because laws vary from one place to another, and your needs are specific to your group, the safest course is to speak to your attorney and at least one insurance agent.

As an ethical matter, rescue groups should provide all volunteers with information about their own need to be insured, again preferably with the advice of an attorney. Volunteers' home owners or renters insurance and their automobile insurance may not cover damages incurred in doing rescue work, so they need to check. They may also want to purchase personal liability insurance, even if your group is incorporated and insured. Finally, anyone engaging in rescue work should have health insurance—even a simple bite can be expensive to treat with antibiotics, and a more serious injury can be financially significant.

CHAPTER

2

Volunteers:
The Hearts of Rescue

Although some people are paid to work with homeless animals, the overwhelming majority of women and men involved with rescue work are volunteers. For many of these, rescue is a central factor in their lives, and a more-than-full-time second job. Others contribute a few hours a month to help the cause. Most rescuers fall somewhere in between. In other words, your role in rescue is what you make it.

But why would you want to give up your evenings and weekends, parts of your home, some of your money, many of your other interests, and huge hunks of your heart to work without pay? Because, among other things, rescue work:

- Improves the lives of individual animals and people.
- Promotes informed, compassionate interaction between people and pets.
- Provides opportunities to learn more about animals and the issues surrounding them.
- Offers opportunities to teach others about animals and the issues surrounding them.
- Contributes in concrete ways to communities by caring for homeless animals and, sometimes, by helping people keep the animals they have.
- Brings animal lovers together and fosters communication and friendship.

- Shows us, in the animals we meet, the power of compassion, patience, forgiveness, and love.

There are countless more good reasons to volunteer with a rescue program, as any experienced rescuer will tell you. There are also countless reasons not to. The joys of the work are often tempered by heartache, stress, and emotional roller coaster rides. Some animals arrive in poor condition, and some are difficult to handle. A few are downright frightening. Rescue work can eat up time and can create conflict with family and friends.

If you're a potential or new rescue volunteer, this chapter is meant to help you make important decisions and dodge some common hazards. If you already work as a rescuer, my hope is that you will periodically step back and reassess your involvement based on the points discussed here. But let's begin by looking at the work itself.

FOSTERING ANIMALS IN TRANSITION

Foster caretakers are central to most rescue programs, few of which have centralized facilities for rescued animals. In fact, many rescuers prefer not to use group shelters for animals because individualized care in home settings has many advantages. Proximity to large groups of animals can be very stressful for individual animals, exacerbating some issues and camouflaging others. Foster homes, in contrast, provide environments like adopters' homes, making evaluation of the animal more accurate and preparing him better for his new home and family. Foster families provide their charges with basic training and are in an ideal position to observe and assess the animals' reactions to children, other pets, men, women, strangers, storms, noise, activity, and other everyday events that could trigger potential problems in an adoptive home. Foster caretakers' observations can be indispensable when it comes time to match the animal to an appropriate adopter.

Before you volunteer to foster, please assess your situation carefully and be realistic. Fostering can be hard work and can disrupt your home life, sometimes in unexpected ways. Introducing "just one more" animal into your home can create chaos during the adjustment period or longer. And although most caretakers never experience a problem, the job is not without risk.

The Risks of Fostering

Health Risks to Your Pets
Your first priority (aside from your human family) should be your own pets. It's all too easy to focus on the needs of an animal who has been neglected or abused to the point that we slight the emotional needs of our own healthy companions. Be sure to

spend some one-on-one time with your pets every day, preferably without the foster animal. Pay attention to your pets' emotions. If you find that bringing strangers into the home, especially one after another, is too stressful for the animals who love you day in and day out, find another way to help rescue. Yes, I know that many groups are desperate for foster homes. Nevertheless, it's simply unethical and cruel to hurt your own pets in the name of charity for others.

Your pets also rely on you to safeguard their physical health. For a more detailed discussion of health issues in rescue, see Chapter 8. Basically, the following steps will help protect your pets:

- Keep their vaccinations or titers current.
- Have fecal specimens checked for intestinal parasites and blood samples checked for heartworm regularly as recommended by your veterinarian.
- Be alert to signs of external parasites, and respond quickly if you see any.
- If possible, take foster animals only after they have been through a quarantine period, or isolate them from your other pets until you are sure they are healthy.
- Clean and disinfect regularly, and ask your vet for advice.

Lost Fosters

It's always possible for a foster animal to escape and become lost, especially if he is nervous, frightened, and new to your home. Foster dogs and cats should wear identification tags, and some groups microchip the animals in their care. Many rescue organizations have tags printed with the group's name and telephone number. If you foster on a regular basis, have a tag made with your name and number as well. That way if a lost foster animal is found, he can be returned either directly to you or to the rescue group.

Safety Issues with Foster Animals

Responsible rescue programs do all they can to keep everyone safe, but volunteers must understand that some behavioral issues may not show up until the animal has been in rescue some time. Besides, what is "dangerous behavior" in one situation may be simply a nuisance—or even acceptable—in another. In a household with very young children or infirm adults, a rambunctious fifty-pound dog may pose serious risks. The same dog in a household with healthy adults and older children may be the perfect jogging/hiking/ball-playing companion. An animal who shows fear-induced aggression may be comfortable in a quiet environment, but a bite or swipe waiting to happen in a loud, busy household. Some animals are cooperative and gentle; others require experienced handlers.

Being a hands-on rescuer carries responsibility not only to the animals in your temporary care, but also to yourself, your human family, your other pets, and any other people or animals who may come within reach of the foster animals in your care. No one should foster, transport, or otherwise handle a rescued animal that seems likely to cause injury, intentional or not. Nor should any volunteer feel embarrassed to decline responsibility for a particular animal.

Messy Foster Animals

Accidents happen, and sooner or later a foster animal will have one at your house. Here are some tips for dealing with clean up (*see* Chapter 9 for more on inappropriate elimination).

- If you catch a spot of urine while it is fresh, clean the spot with detergent or carpet shampoo, then soak it with club soda for about ten minutes and blot. Follow with white vinegar or an enzyme product designed to neutralize odor.
- Remove urine on launderable items by washing once in the machine with a cup of vinegar in the water, then again as usual with detergent.
- Urine fluoresces in longwave UV light (black light), so to find invisible urine spots, use a UV lamp, preferably one with a filter for extraneous light. Most hardware stores carry reasonably priced black lights. Clean the area as described above. (If the urine has soaked through the carpet and pad and into the floor below, it will be difficult to deodorize the carpet no matter what you use. It may be necessary to remove the old carpet, clean and seal the underfloor, and then re-cover with carpet or a non-absorbent surface).
- If you foster animals who slobber or lick a lot, be aware that the enzymes in saliva can stain clothes, ceilings, walls, and tabletops. For washable fabrics, wet the spots and sprinkle them liberally with meat tenderizer. Let it soak for a few minutes, then wash as usual. For other surfaces, use appropriate cleaning products.
- To clean feces and vomit, begin by removing as much as you can. Then clean the area with detergent (Dawn dish detergent works well) or another cleaner made for the surface you are cleaning. Finally, apply an enzymatic cleaning product, following the directions for best results.

Several excellent products for removing organic odors are on the market—Nature's Miracle, Simple Solution, Outright!, and Resolve reportedly work well. Another, Odor Mute, leaves a white residue but works on concrete. Enzymes in these products break down the odor-causing compounds in urine, feces, and vomit. Follow product directions closely for best results.

Disposal of feces can become a problem for homes with several pets and foster animals. Check your local ordinances concerning waste removal, and be environmentally conscious. If you or your neighbors get your household water from wells, improper waste disposal could contaminate the water supply, and in any case, improperly handled waste matter will contaminate groundwater and leach into streams and rivers. In urban and suburban areas, improper disposal can be a nuisance and a health hazard, and some waste disposal companies prohibit or limit disposal of animal waste with garbage. If disposal is a problem, talk to area businesses that house animals—veterinarians, boarding kennels, training facilities, and groomers. Ask them for ideas before you begin fostering—don't let the problem literally pile up on you!

Working with Foster Animals

Many rescued animals have behavioral issues ranging from almost insignificant to seriously annoying or even dangerous (*see* Chapter 9). If you volunteer to foster animals, or to work with them in other ways, be realistic about your ability to manage and retrain the less-than-model citizens. There's no shame in saying that you don't have the time or skills to handle certain problems, and you won't do anyone any favors by taking on an animal whose behavior is too much for you. Keep learning and improving your training skills, and you may be ready for the next problem child.

Be realistic, too, about the impact that a particular animal may have on other members of your family, human and non-human alike. If you have an elderly dog, a rambunctious adolescent canine rescue may be too much for the old guy physically and emotionally. The same for an elderly cat and an energetic kitten. People, too, can be overwhelmed physically and emotionally by certain animals, so be fair to your human family when you take on foster animals.

When the Time Comes: Letting Go of Foster Pets

The departure of a rescued animal from his foster home is a bittersweet occasion. Foster caretakers and their families develop very close attachments to the animals in their charge, and the animals to them. And yet, something astonishing happens when adopters pick up their new pets. Perhaps they read our minds and hearts, but somehow, the animals seem to know. I've seen many a clingy foster animal leap into an adopter's car and leave without a backward glance. It's that leap of faith and hope that all rescuers work to achieve.

Keep tissues nearby, and remember that you are not losing a friend, but making new ones. Take a deep breath, then clean everything up so you'll be ready for the next rescued animal who needs love and safe harbor on his journey home.

I CAN'T TAKE IN ANIMALS — WHAT <u>CAN</u> I DO?

Not all rescue volunteers foster animals. Here, thanks to members of my on-line rescue discussion list, are some other volunteer jobs that contribute to the rescue effort in important ways, beginning with jobs that involve non-fostering contact with animals:

* **Spotters** or **shelter liaisons** check shelters for animals that come under the rescue group's umbrella and develop good working relationships with shelter staff to facilitate transfer of animals to the rescue group.

- **Transporters** transport animals long and short distances, often coordinating with other rescue groups for mutual benefit.
- **Trainers** who have the experience and skills to help with behavior issues can work with animals on a regular basis, and advise and train foster caretakers to reinforce the training between sessions.

Other volunteer positions require no direct contact with the animals, including the following:

- **Application screeners** read adoption applications and sometimes speak to applicants, then pass along their insights, observations, and recommendations to the person or committee in charge of adoptions.
- **Volunteer coordinators** field inquiries from potential volunteers, organize and sometimes conduct training sessions, help fit volunteers to jobs, and follow up to keep things running smoothly.
- **Foster home coordinators** match up rescued animals and foster homes, and stay in touch to be sure that all is well.
- **Archivists** or **Historians** maintain records, ensuring that they are complete and up-to-date.
- **Professional consultants** offer advice and, sometimes, *pro bono* or reduced-fee services in their areas of expertise—a perfect way for busy lawyers, insurance specialists, veterinarians, tax consultants, and others to contribute as needed.
- **Fundraisers** coordinate and create opportunities to raise money and acquire material goods essential to running a rescue program.
- **Computer gurus** help with a variety of computer-related activities, ranging from setting up data bases for records to designing and maintaining web sites, on-line stores, blogs, discussion groups, and so on. Simply keeping postings on such sites can be a big job.
- **Contact people** field calls and e-mails regarding pets in need and other matters, handling some and referring others to the right individuals. This works rather like an operator or receptionist for a business, helping to reduce the work load on other rescuers and to lower the frustration level as people try to reach the right person.
- **Publicists** and **Public relations specialists** spread the word about rescue by writing and distributing media releases and written materials and by setting up appearances at malls, libraries, festivals, and other public events. They may also be able to arrange for veterinarians, groomers, kennels, and trainers to provide services at a reduced rate in exchange for publicity.
- **Home visitors** can visit adoption applicants prior to adoptions and possibly for post-adoption follow-ups.
- **Writers** and **Researchers** can generate or acquire (in compliance with copyright laws, please) handouts of use to current pet owners and potential adopters.

- **Artists, Authors**, and **Crafters** may contribute items for fund raisers or donate all or part of the proceeds from sales made through a rescue group. (For instance, I regularly contribute to rescue and other animal-related causes from sales both of my books and my paintings). Galleries and art or craft groups may also be willing to hold a benefit show or sale.
- **Photographers** can photograph animals available for adoption; take photos of rescue events, volunteers, and successfully adopted pets; and take photos of pets at fund raising events.

BEFORE YOU LEAP: PITFALLS OF RESCUE WORK

The last thing I want to do is discourage anyone from helping the rescue cause. But it is important to be realistic about the hazards that come with the work, and to consider carefully which risks you can and should accept.

Legal and Financial Liability for Rescuers

In their eagerness to help animals, many people don't consider their potential legal and financial liability. If you simply pick up an occasional stray and find him a new home, your risk is probably low. But if you work with a rescue group, or if you rescue animals on a regular basis on your own, the risk increases.

For one thing, the more animals you handle, the more chance that one of them will do something that injures someone or damages property while in your care or afterward. You, and the group with which you work, could be sued, and even if you prevail, defending a lawsuit can be very expensive. In rare cases, you could be held criminally liable as well. Here are some suggestions:

- Know the laws of the areas where you operate. If you are uncertain about how a particular law or ordinance affects you as a rescuer, consult an attorney.
- Ask for a copy of any insurance policy carried by the rescue group with which you work, and ask to be kept informed of any changes in the coverage. Specifically, find out whether all volunteers are covered, or just board members. Many groups do not carry insurance, and you need to know one way or the other.
- Check the coverage of your homeowners' and automobile insurance, and ask specifically if you are covered for damages caused by a foster animal or while driving on rescue business. Some people may advise you to stay mum, but doing so could leave you financially vulnerable, potentially endangering your home and other assets.
- Ask your attorney whether you should carry personal liability insurance.

Forewarned is forearmed, and knowing where you stand legally will let you make informed decisions about where to apply your talents to support rescue.

When the death of a North Carolina breeder left a large number of dogs homeless, rescuers from the Cocker Spaniel Adoption Center traveled from Maryland to help. Rescuers Rob and Nancy Klein decided to stretch the definition of "Cocker rescue" and took the one non-spaniel in the group, a big yellow apparently Lab-Beagle cross, back to Maryland to an all-breed rescue program. Volunteer Linda Coleman took the dog home to foster, fell in love, and adopted him, illustrating one of the hazards of rescue work! With the stable environment and obedience training, Riley has blossomed into a world-class charmer. Friendly and always eager to please, he quickly qualified as a therapy dog. Riley enjoys visiting a local nursing home and frequently helps with pet care presentations for local schools and organizations. In his spare time, he hangs out with Linda and Dudley (see Chapter 10). Photo by Sheila Boneham.

What Can You Afford to Do?

Money can certainly be a factor in deciding what you can volunteer to do. Some rescue jobs will cost you little or no money, but others can become costly in no time. If you can afford to spend a little money on behalf of the animals without adding to your credit card debt or causing money fights at home, that's fine. But if your financial resources are limited, then be sensible about what jobs you take on, and be sure you understand clearly what the group will pay for and what you are expected to cover yourself. For example:

- If your job involves long-distance calling, will you be reimbursed or provided with a calling card or cell phone?

- If you foster animals, are you expected to pay for their food and other daily supplies? What about crates or cages, bedding, toys, collars, and so on?
- If you need to transport an animal, will you be reimbursed for travel? This is probably not an issue for short trips to the vet or obedience class but can become an issue if you regularly drive long distances for rescue.
- If you take an animal to the veterinarian or groomer, are you expected to pay the bill to be reimbursed, or have other arrangements been made? If you are to be reimbursed, what are the procedures, and how long can you expect to wait to receive your money?
- How are emergency expenses handled? Animal emergencies always seem to occur on Saturday night, and many emergency clinics are expensive and require payment in advance of treatment. If you are fostering, you need to know not only how emergency expenses are handled, but who can authorize payment for high-cost procedures, and how and when that authorization can be made.

Here's the bottom line for volunteers, and for groups recruiting volunteers: No volunteer should be expected to incur financial obligations that are beyond her means to handle easily and willingly. In other words, no one should go into debt in order to give, and no one's family or pets should do without the things they need because the money has been spent on rescue. Charity begins at home.

Is Your Family Enthusiastic About Rescue?

Not all members of your household have to be equally enthusiastic about your rescue work, but if they are openly hostile to the idea, that may affect the duties you can take on, the amount of time you can spend, and your state of mind as you do the work. If you plan to foster, you need the acceptance and support of everyone in your household. The last thing a rescued animal needs is to experience additional stress from human conflict or hostility.

On the other hand, if your family members support your work and like animals, they can help provide the sort of stable, nurturing environment that helps foster animals make the journey to their new homes. If you have children, be sure they understand that the animals in their care won't be their pets forever. Be prepared, too, for the foster that someone—or everyone!—falls in love with. The urge to adopt is a common hazard for foster caretakers.

Finally, be aware of how your own pet or pets respond to the presence of a foster animal and his eventual departure. Your pet's personality, size, energy level, age, and sex may affect which foster animals you can accommodate. Some pets also become attached to foster animals and can become depressed or anxious when fosters leave.

BURNOUT

Rescuing and rehoming animals has many rewards, as we've seen. But the work is definitely work, and the emotional and physical toll it takes on volunteers can be high. As in various types of human social work, burnout is very common among rescue volunteers, especially those who work in "high-volume" breeds or species. Some burned out rescuers take sabbaticals or quit for good. Others keep going, many for longer than they should.

There's an axiom that says that you cannot help others if you don't take care of yourself, and the principle applies well to rescue work. If you are a volunteer, you must take proper care of yourself (and your family and pets) before you can take proper care of needy animals and the people involved with them. You cannot do that if you are burned out from the effort. If you manage volunteers, you owe it to them and to your group to recognize signs of burnout and to "rescue" those who show them.

What are the signs of burnout? They vary, of course, depending on the individual's personality, situation, and experience, but may include chronic physical exhaustion, depression, a sense of hopelessness, anger, and, often, impatience with and lack of compassion for people with "pet problems."

Solutions to the burnout problem also vary widely, but here are some suggestions that may help prevent burnout from occurring, or "cure" it when it does.

- Understand that the existence of homeless animals is not new and is not likely to go away any time soon. Neither is ignorance, nor incidents of neglect or outright cruelty. Accept that you cannot rescue every animal, and you cannot reform most people. Do what you can, but don't suffer for what you cannot do.
- Be realistic about what you can do to help. If you cannot foster animals, so be it. If you have as many pets in your home as you can manage responsibly or as many as the law allows, don't take "just one more." If you can do nothing else, you can donate money or goods to a rescue group, and that's really quite a lot.
- Realize that you are not the only person who can take good care of animals. (If you think you are, or that no one else does it properly, it's definitely time for you to take a break.)
- When you need to say no, say no. Don't feel obligated to explain or make excuses. Simply say, "Thank you for thinking of me, but at this time I have to say no." If you can recommend someone else, do so, but don't feel that you must.
- Don't give up the rest of your life for rescue. Keep your priorities straight. Rescued animals are important, but so are your own pets, your family, your friends, your job, and your health. Make rescue part of your life, not your whole life. Have fun!
- Take part in or spectate at other sorts of animal-oriented activities—canine obedience trials, cat agility competitions, whatever. Get to know responsible breeders,

fanciers, and trainers, and listen to their perspectives on animal-related issues. If all your ideas come from just one corner of the world, you won't have the information you need to form logical opinions. Spend time with happy animals and their people.

- Trust your colleagues to do their work, even if their style is different from yours. Don't try to micromanage other people's efforts.
- Be as kind to people as you are to animals. Be slow to judge, avoid gossip, and shun "shark fests." The reasons people give for relinquishing their pets are often only part of the story. What you hear from gossips may be wrong. And in this electronic world of ours, accusations passed from person to person, or list to list on the Internet, may be way off base. Focus your efforts and emotions on positive action, not on anger and (possibly false or exaggerated) accusations. Educate the people who will learn, realize that some won't, and move on.
- Ask for help and financial support when you need them. If you don't ask, other people may not realize you need anything.
- Accept that some animals simply cannot be rehomed due to health, temperament, or behavioral issues, and understand that humane euthanasia is sometimes the most responsible way to rescue such animals from pain and suffering.
- Quit when you need to, for a week, a month, a year. You can always come back to rescue work later if you want to, or you may find other ways to contribute to society. Humbling though it may be, realize that you aren't indispensable, and rescue work will continue without you.

CHAPTER

3

Finding, Training, and Managing Volunteers

Volunteers are the heart of animal rescue. A very small minority of rescue groups have paid employees, but for the vast majority, volunteers do the work. They screen, transport, bathe, groom, evaluate, nurse, train, house, and rehabilitate animals. They answer phones and e-mails, staff information tables, screen adopters, and raise money and material support. Clearly, the best interest of a rescue group is served by finding ways to attract and hang on to good volunteers.

If your organization is new, you may count your members on one hand, but as your visibility increases, those few people won't be able to do everything that needs to be done—nor should they (more on that later). If you work in a group that has been around awhile and has a larger network of volunteers already, it's a good idea to solicit regular feedback from the troops and reassess how you manage, train, and motivate your current volunteers and attract new ones. That's what this chapter is about.

WHERE ARE YOU NOW?

One of your goals should be to expand, diversify, and organize your volunteer base so that the same few people aren't stuck with all of the work, and any volunteer can take a break or leave without the program falling apart. As you expand beyond your initial handful of volunteers, you need to elect or appoint a volunteer coordinator (*see* Chapter 1), who may or may not be a voting member of the BOD. Her job is to recruit and evaluate potential volunteers, arrange for their initial and in-service training, assign them specific duties, match animals with foster homes, and help design and implement ways to reward and motivate them. Your volunteer coordinator needs to have excellent people skills, including the ability to listen carefully, communicate clearly, compromise when appropriate, and stand strong when necessary.

Take a look at the volunteers you already have. Who are they and how did they become associated with your rescue program? Are they pet owners who love the breed or species? Perhaps adopters who want to help the effort? Are they breeders who see rescue as a way to give something back to their breed? Diversity among your volunteers will strengthen your organization because different people bring different strengths, knowledge, and skills to the group.

Ask your volunteers why they do rescue work and why they chose to work with *your* program. Ask long-term volunteers why they continue, and if you can do it diplomatically, ask former volunteers why they quit or changed groups. If possible, exchange information with other rescue groups, shelters, and even non-animal-oriented volunteer programs to learn why people volunteer. Knowing the psychology of volunteerism can help you attract good volunteers and hang onto them.

Identify the jobs that must be done to make the program work. Divide your list into critical and supporting tasks. *Critical* tasks are those without which there would be no rescues: screening and transporting animals, fostering animals and/or referring potential adopters to owners, screening potential adopters, and matching animals with adopters. *Supporting* tasks facilitate the fundamental work of rescue, and include publicity, public education, fund-raising, coordination of group activities, and whatever other activities your group thinks appropriate.

Although you can refer to your people simply as "volunteers," as your group expands you may find it helpful to distinguish the duties of different people with job titles and descriptions. Spell out the responsibilities and limitations of each type of position, leaving enough wriggle room to accommodate unusual situations (which seem to be the norm in rescue work). Spelling out what needs to be done and who is able and willing to do it will let you make better use of your volunteers. Having clear guidelines from which to work will make your volunteers more confident and productive, and will help them figure out who to go to for information or action beyond their own duties or abilities. Once you've defined your present volunteers' status and figured out the jobs that need to be done, it's time to start your recruitment campaign.

RECRUITING VOLUNTEERS

Rescue volunteers are as diverse as the animals they serve. Many are deeply immersed in the fancy as breeders or competitors; some make their livings from pet-oriented fields like veterinary medicine, grooming, or training. Some of the best volunteers simply love animals. The trick for rescue organizers is to find potential volunteers and to help them find you.

To begin, draft several standard statements you can use to let people know that you need volunteers. Here are some ideas:

- A short, sweet version—"Volunteers Needed" or "Foster Homes Needed." You can run notices with just these two or three words, your group's name, and contact information (phone number, e-mail address, or web site) in various publications. You can also make signs to attract people to talk to volunteers or pick up literature at public events.
- A paragraph-length version to use where appropriate—on web sites, perhaps, or in magazines, newspapers, or show catalogs, or as occasional media releases (*see* Chapter 5).
- A detailed version describing your organization, and exactly what volunteers do. Many people think they would have to foster or handle animals to help, so this detailed description of volunteer opportunities is your chance to recruit people for other jobs. (*See* Chapter 2 for ideas.)

Because volunteers come from all walks of life, and many are not involved in any other formal aspects of the pet fancy, you should cast a wide net for volunteers. You may be able to place free notices in some cases, but a modest promotional budget can get you a lot of exposure if you plan carefully. Even if you don't get new volunteers right away, you increase awareness of your organization in particular and rescue in general. Here are some outlets to consider for your recruiting notices:

- Your web site.
- E-mail discussion lists and/or appropriate blogs.
- Local newspapers and magazines.
- Free regional pet tabloids or magazines distributed through pet supply stores, kennels, groomers, training facilities, and other outlets.
- Newsletters put out by clubs and registries for breeders, competitors, and other enthusiasts.
- Bulletin boards at veterinary offices, pet supply stores, grooming and boarding facilities, and even non-animal businesses that offer community bulletin boards.
- If you need to recruit a volunteer with a specific skill, try targeted advertising. Need a volunteer bookkeeper? Try a notice at an accounting firm or a local business school. Need a writer to make your literature look and sound professional? Try a local college English or journalism department (you might even be able to set up an unpaid internship).

Before the applications start pouring in, I have one more suggestion. Encourage your current volunteers to write down their own reasons for being involved in rescue work, and your rescue group in particular. You're on the hook for this, too. After all, you can't expect to attract volunteers to work that is often frustrating, heartbreaking, and downright difficult if you can't explain the rewards.

This charming smile belongs to Olive Oink, a Vietnamese pot-bellied pig who was dropped into the night box at the Fort Wayne Animal Control shelter when she was twelve weeks old. Andrea and David Cole, who had owned another pot-bellied pig, began by fostering Olive and treating her mange. Andrea explains that some people purchase pot-bellied piglets as novel pets or status symbols, but soon realize that although the pigs are very smart, they are not dogs. Many pigs have been dumped and euthanized at shelters or turned loose. No adopter surfaced for Olive, who is the cutest, sweetest creature you can imagine, but definitely not a suitable pet for most people or environments. At a hundred pounds, grown-up Olive gets along great with the Cole's sighthounds (and, with a healthy porcine self-image, she does not covet their svelte figures). Olive enjoys keeping the fenced yard of her country home free of dandelions, and she will "work" for cheese puffs and carrots (see Chapter 9). Olive nestles into her blanketed "pen" in the foyer of the Cole's home in cold weather, and sleeps in her outdoor "pigloo" in the summer. Exotic pets like Olive need very special rescuers and adopters, but all of us can help educate people about making realistic pet choices. PHOTO BY SHEILA BONEHAM.

SCREENING POTENTIAL VOLUNTEERS

Taking on volunteers is something of a balancing act. You need enough hands to make the work a little lighter, but those hands must be attached to people with whom you are happy to work. The reputation and success of your entire rescue program, and of animal rescue in general, rests with the people you empower to speak and act on behalf of your group. Clearly, you need to screen all potential volunteers.

Before you can screen applicants effectively, you need to define the jobs that need to be done and the skills and traits needed to do them. Then you need to establish your volunteer policies. Will you verify information given by applicants? Visit their homes to see their own pets? Will you allow foster caretakers to adopt animals in their care? Will you accept applicants who breed or show animals, or those who belong to groups with extreme positions regarding animals?

Next, you need to develop an application form. Most groups find they need a written version, and many also use an on-line version on their web sites. The application should include questions that identify people's skills and interests and collect the information related to your volunteer policies (e.g., "What animal-related organizations do you belong to or support?" or "Please describe your history as a pet owner").

If you have specific volunteer positions available, give written job descriptions to the applicant along with the application. Many rescue jobs, such as fostering, checking shelters, and staffing information tables, are always open because there never seem to be enough people to do the jobs. Opportunities for more specialized positions, such as treasurer/bookkeeper, webmaster, or newsletter editor, are limited.

After your volunteer coordinator has reviewed the written application, she should arrange to interview the applicant. Face-to-face interviews are ideal, but if your group covers a large geographic area, telephone interviews can also work. The written application gives you one kind of information, but you need to meet or at least speak to potential volunteers to get a feel for their individual communication styles. One person may be brilliant at handling animals, but not so good with people—so not the best person to speak to the public or interact with animal-shelter staffs. Another may be a gifted speaker and talented fund raiser who lacks the skills to handle any but the most cooperative and docile animals. Each of them can make valuable contributions to the rescue effort. Your volunteer coordinator's task is to figure who can and should do which job.

People's personalities, interests, and skills may vary, but good volunteers do share some important traits. Some of these traits will quickly become apparent in your first meeting; others may not be obvious at first. In general, a good volunteer answers questions about her qualifications and background willingly, communicates well, is enthusiastic and committed, and relates easily to the interviewer. Beware of rigidly opinionated and controlling types. These people may be dedicated to the cause and may work hard, but they will be difficult to work with and may antagonize people you want as your allies. There are many shades of gray in the world of rescue, and people who see every issue in black and white often do more harm than good. The best volunteer is flexible, because animals don't need help on a predictable schedule and don't have their medical emergencies at convenient times. And although rescue is serious work, a sense of humor is a major asset.

If a volunteer holds beliefs and attitudes that diverge widely from the policies and philosophy of your organization, or if she appears to have a hidden agenda, it will be difficult to impossible to nurture a comfortable working relationship with her. Suppose, for instance, that your group supports responsible breeding and encourages informed purchases of responsibly bred animals in addition to adoption. A volunteer who opposes all breeding and bad-mouths all breeders won't endear you to the breeders, organizations, and owners of responsibly bred animals who might otherwise support and work with you, nor is her position in the best interest of animals. The flip side is that the volunteer herself won't be comfortable if she feels her own beliefs are compromised by working under your group's policies.

Any person who wants to handle animals as part of her volunteer work must be screened with special care, whether she hopes to foster, screen shelter animals, transport animals, or interact with animals in some other capacity. Someone from your group (preferably the volunteer coordinator or an officer or board member) should arrange to visit the applicant's home to meet her own pets and see how they live. If she can't or doesn't choose to care for her own pets properly, why would you entrust foster animals to her? If she seems to mean well, you may be able to help her become better educated about pet care, but if there is any sign of abuse or neglect, don't take her on.

You also need to observe the applicant with animals she hasn't met before—several of them if possible. You might do this when you interview her, or arrange a special "animal interview" after you've checked out her own pets. This will give your volunteer coordinator a chance to assess how the applicant relates to animals in general, how well she seems to read their body language, and how skilled she is at managing animals with minimal training or other issues, as well as how animals respond to her. If the applicant has a family and wants to foster animals, someone needs to meet all members of the household and see how they interact with strange animals, too. It's important to know each volunteer's strengths and limitations so that interactions with animals will be as successful, safe, and productive as possible for everyone involved.

Sooner or later you will have to turn someone down. Whatever your reason, be diplomatic, but don't string people along. Simply tell them that you don't have a position that can make use of their skills. If you think it's appropriate, suggest alternative volunteer opportunities, but don't take on a volunteer you feel is a bad fit for your group.

When you do welcome a new volunteer, you need to be certain that her responsibilities are clearly spelled out, preferably in writing, and that she understands what she may *not* do or say on behalf of the organization. Volunteers who handle animals, whether for a half-hour drive to the vet or month-long fostering, should sign an agreement that clearly states that they are temporary caretakers who agree to surrender animals owned by the group on demand.

ORGANIZING, TRAINING, AND EMPOWERING VOLUNTEERS

Coordinating Volunteers

The job of coordinating volunteers is one of the most important in your group. At first, it may be just one of several jobs that a particular person does, but as your group grows, the job may become big enough to be a person's sole organizational responsibility. The volunteer coordinator needs to be organized, reliable, accessible, responsive, and diplomatic—she'll be working with people, after all. She needs to be knowledgeable about the rescue program, the community, and the animals. She needs creative problem-solving skills and the patience of a saint so she can stay sane when her foster homes are full, she has three fosters herself, and the volunteer who begged for another foster needs "someone" to pick the animal up because she's leaving in the morning for a week in Tahiti. The coordinator should also keep careful records of the good that volunteers do so their contributions can be acknowledged.

Your volunteer coordinator will assign volunteers to specific jobs and give them feedback, both positive and constructively negative. Knowledge is, as they say, power, and the coordinator can help empower your volunteers by organizing materials and events that will help them learn what they need to know to do their jobs and represent your group well.

Tools for Volunteers

A volunteer manual, given to each volunteer and updated as necessary, is invaluable. Not only does it give the individual the information she needs, but it helps ensure that all members of the organization are using the same game plan. That goes a long way to reduce conflict, confusion, and frustration. The manual should include the following materials and any supplemental information that you want to include:

- Your group's mission statement, history, goals, and programs (adoption, fostering, public education, breeder referral, and so on).
- Copies of publications your group distributes (pamphlets, brochures, other handouts).
- Names, titles, telephone numbers, and e-mail addresses of officers and members of the board of directors.
- Names, titles, telephone numbers, and e-mail addresses of the other volunteers. If your group covers a large geographic area, include each person's general location.
- Copies of all forms your group uses, and directions for using each one (adoption applications, fostering and volunteer applications, relinquishment forms).

- Reimbursement policies and procedures.
- Adoption policies and procedures.
- Policies and procedures for receiving animals.
- Policies and procedures for attempting to find owners of strays and for releasing strays back to owners.
- Health and safety precautions.
- Emergency procedures, and names, addresses, and telephone numbers of veterinarians used by the rescue program.
- If you are a purebred rescue program, a copy of the Breed Standard for your breed, along with photographs illustrating variations, including pets with neglected grooming or funny haircuts that make them hard to recognize.
- A list of recommended reading.

A three-ring binder using standard 8½-x-11-inch paper makes it easy for each volunteer to update the manual and to add supplemental materials of her own. Just be sure to leave enough margin to accommodate the holes without chopping out information.

A manual serves as a starting point and reference, but it's not enough to just hand people a book. Fortunately, education is a win-win proposition—you get more benefit from volunteers who are knowledgeable, and your volunteers develop confidence in their own abilities and a sense of belonging that keeps them with the group longer.

Educating Your Volunteers

If you screen your applicants carefully, all your volunteers will come into your ranks with a love for animals and the desire to help, but they won't all have the knowledge and experience they need to be most effective. Granted, some of the burden of becoming educated should and does rest with the individual volunteer. Still, one purpose of every rescue group should be to educate people, and education begins at home, with your own volunteers.

Volunteer education has two phases: immediate and long-term. Let's begin with the information and materials each volunteer needs right away to do her work. Each new volunteer should receive a letter of welcome that clearly outlines what the volunteer is authorized to do on behalf of the rescue program, and to whom she should report. She should also receive a copy of the volunteer manual, or, if you don't yet have one, copies of all forms and materials you regularly use or distribute.

Ideally, new volunteers should come together for a face-to-face orientation session. If your group is small and takes on new people only occasionally, the orientation may be one-on-one with the volunteer coordinator and/or with the person to whom the volunteer will report. If your group is larger and takes on new volunteers frequently, it may be more efficient to hold orientation sessions either when you have a certain number of new volunteers, or at regular intervals. The orientation should cover at least the following topics:

- Basics: the group's purpose, geographic range, organizational structure, policies, and procedures.
- The different kinds of volunteer jobs and what each entails. Everyone should have some idea of what the other volunteers are up to.
- Safety issues. This is, of course, most pertinent for the volunteers who assess, transport, and foster animals, but all volunteers need to be aware.
- Insurance and risk. If your group does not offer insurance for your volunteers (most do not), your volunteers should be encouraged to check their own coverage.
- Potential legal liability (consult an attorney). The idea is not to frighten people, but it is important that people understand that rescue work is not all fluffy kittens and sweet old dogs. Your attorney can offer advice on ways to minimize legal liability.
- What to do in "delicate" situations, which may involve belligerent or uncooperative people, aggressive or hard-to-handle animals, or just downright odd things that pop up from time to time.
- Working relationships with other people and groups, including veterinarians, shelters, other rescue programs, organizations, and businesses.

After the general topics are covered, each volunteer should meet with the person to whom she will report. This meeting may or may not take place at the same time and place as the orientation, depending on what the volunteer will be doing.

If possible, each volunteer should work with a more experienced member of your group initially. This is especially important if she will be working directly with the animals. For the welfare of everyone, human and nonhuman, you need to be sure that each volunteer is competent and confident handling the animals. You can't assess her hands-on abilities in an interview or application form.

No one's education is ever complete, least of all in regard to our relations with animals, so every rescue program should, if possible, offer on-going education opportunities for all its members. If your group is small or lacks the resources to sponsor educational sessions, team up with other groups. Assign one of your volunteers to identify learning opportunities offered by area vets, trainers, shelters, organizations, and animal-oriented businesses and make the information available to your volunteers.

Rescuers benefit from learning about the obvious topics—nutrition, health and safety, behavior, and species- or breed-specific topics. What may not be so obvious is that we and the animals we rescue also benefit when volunteers learn about other breeds and other kinds of animals.

Education Isn't Just for People

One of the biggest reasons that animals are relinquished to rescue programs and shelters by their owners is lack of training. I make that statement ambiguous on purpose, because many people who have untrained animals are themselves un-trained. They don't know how to train their pets, and some don't seem to know that their animals could be trained. Unfortunately, way too many rescuers are also ignorant about animal training. Please see to it that your people are a cut above. If you are a dog rescue group, encourage (dare I say require?) every one of your members to take a dog (their own or a foster dog) through at least one good obedience class. If the volunteer is physically unable to participate in training, or if you rescue a non-canine species, encourage your volunteers nev-ertheless to observe a training class (which will most likely involve dogs). The species may be different, but positive training methods work on nearly all ani-mals (including volunteers!).

If you can find a place to hold training sessions and presentations, consider open-ing them to volunteers from other rescue groups as well as to your adopters and even pos-sibly the public. They should ideally be free for your own volunteers and adopters, but you might charge a small fee for other people to defray any costs you incur and to benefit your organization. Many speakers will donate their time, and well-known individuals who charge a fee usually also attract a bigger audience. Here are some possibilities:

- Veterinarians or veterinary technicians
- Behaviorists or trainers
- Groomers
- Shelter personnel
- Your attorney
- Your insurance consultant
- Experienced fund raisers from other not-for-profit groups
- Authors—me, for instance!

Reward, Motivate, and Empower Your Volunteers

Many of the rewards of rescue work are inherent in the work itself. They lie in the re-lief that comes when you take an animal out of a bad situation, or help a good person who can't care for a pet for reasons beyond his control. They lie, too, in the visceral pleasure of seeing an animal blossom in a safe environment, and in the happiness brought about by a successful placement. They lie in the sense of belonging to a com-munity of like-minded colleagues that circles the earth.

Still, there are things that your group can do to expand the rewards for your vol-unteers, and empower them to be more effective. Your group's relationship with vol-unteers should always benefit both. Because volunteer work is altruistic and unpaid, some organizations treat volunteers as selfless beings who require nothing in return for their work. The fact is, though, that volunteers need and deserve to be rewarded for their contributions. Many of the rewards, of course, are intangible, but they are nevertheless real and valuable. If they weren't, most people wouldn't be masochistic enough to do the work, especially once they've stepped into the hard realities of animal abuse, ignorance, and necessary euthanasia—not to mention bodily fluids on the carpet.

Rewards needn't bite into your budget. Many, in fact, cost no money at all. Here are some ideas:

- *Introduce your volunteers and boost their credibility*: Anyone who represents your group to vets, shelters, and businesses should have a *letter of introduction* signed by the president or volunteer coordinator, and *business cards* to hand out. Letters should identify the individual; cards may or may not be possible, depending on your budget and needs. (You can print your own cards, or try VistaPrint.com for inexpensive printing.)
- *Identify your volunteers*: Provide ID tags when you hold public events (first name only, or just "Volunteer" to protect their privacy). When you gather for meetings, training sessions, or other group-only events, provide name tags to make it easier for people to get to know one another.
- *Educate your volunteers* as discussed earlier in this chapter.
- *Tickle and stroke your volunteers*: Hold a picnic or dinner. If you can, and if appropriate for your species, include available and adopted animals. Invite adopters and donors as well as volunteers and their families. Bestow inexpensive awards, serious and humorous.
- *Thank your volunteers*: Send thank you notes (by mail, not e-mail) to the volunteer and her family whenever a foster animal moves on. It's important to acknowledge the contributions of families, because they support the volunteers' rescue efforts, put up with whatever havoc the foster animals wreak, and shed tears when animals leave.

The time and effort you spend to recruit and select the best possible volunteers, and to train, motivate, support, empower, and reward them, will more than repay you. We become involved with rescue work because we love animals, but we must always remember that our work is about animals *and people*.

CHAPTER

4

Financial and Material Support

Money and material resources are essential rescue tools. Without them, serious rescue work is impossible. Your group does not need to maintain a big bank balance, but does need sufficient money and equipment to transport animals as needed, feed them and care for them properly, pay for the services of veterinarians and possibly other professionals, and so on. If you want to expand your efforts to public education (*see* Chapters 5 and 11), you will need money or outside support. Most important, and assuming you have enough volunteers to do the work, having adequate funding will enable you to support individual animals longer and to be more discriminating in rehoming them.

There are many ways to raise money, and many excellent sources of information on fund raising for not-for-profit organizations. Start with the basics, and don't be afraid to look for new sources of money and supplies. Talk to volunteers from other rescue programs and other types of charities about their fund raising successes and failures. Keep your eyes open for more possibilities, and be creative. The ideas in this chapter are based on my own experience and on input from experienced rescuers around the country.

NOT-FOR-PROFIT AND TAX-EXEMPT STATUS

Designation by the IRS as a 501c not-for-profit corporation will provide advantages for your group (*see* Chapter 1). It will also make you more attractive to donors, who can claim tax deductions for gifts of money, goods, and professional services. Many companies will match their employees' donations to not-for-profit groups, so ask all your adopters, volunteers, and donors to find out whether their employers have matching grant programs. Talk about an everybody wins situation! Your organization raises more money, the adopters and volunteers feel good about helping the effort and get "credit" at work for giving to charity, and their employers gain tax advantages and public relations opportunities. Above all, the animals benefit.

Your group may also qualify for certain tax benefits at the state and local levels, including exemptions from sales and other taxes. To take full advantage of the laws where you live, check state, local, and federal regulations and consult an attorney or accountant—preferably one who will donate some services.

RAISING MONEY

Rescue organizations raise money from two major sources: donations, and sales of goods and/or services. Some of the sources are obvious—adoption and other donations, or sales of pet-related items, for instance. With some imagination, though, you can create other opportunities to make money and raise awareness at the same time.

Adoption Donations

One of the first and most important decisions you need to make is how much adopters must pay to adopt an animal from your group, and what you will call that payment. Most rescue groups have an adoption fee or adoption donation. "Donation" is a useful term for several reasons. It has a psychological edge over "fee," as people are happier donating to a worthwhile cause than they are paying a fee. A donation reinforces the fact that you are not in the business of selling animals for profit, but of taking in and rehoming animals in need. And, as I noted earlier, some adopters work for companies that will match charitable donations. Finally, people who don't mind *donating* more than asked rarely want to *pay* more than the stated fee.

The minimum adoption donation should be high enough to speak to the value of the animal and the adopter's commitment, but not be so high that it drives adopters away. The donation should cover the expenses of your typical rescued animal, but not necessarily extraordinary costs incurred by special cases. A standard minimum donation based on an average is more fair to adopters than donations designed to cover the individual animal's expenses. Standard donations also benefit the animals, because each of them should be placed to fit the adopter's needs, experience, and life-style (*see* Chapter 10), not the adopter's ability to cover that animal's expenses.

You can calculate your average cost per animal by totaling your expenses and dividing by the number of animals you have rescued altogether, or if you've been at it for a long time, the past couple of years. If you are new to rescue, you can estimate what you will spend per "average" animal by adding up your likely expenses, including:

- Food.
- Equipment and supplies (grooming equipment, shampoo, crates or cages, leashes, collars or harnesses, toys, and so on).
- Veterinary care and supplies (vet visits, altering if paid by your group, vaccinations, parasite control products, preventative medications, and so on);
- Other professional services (groomers, trainers, or behaviorists, and so on).
- Transportation costs (even if you don't reimburse your volunteers for transporting animals, you should calculate the cost of doing so).
- Support costs, including telephone and Internet expenses, advertising, printing or copying, and so on.
- Other items included with the animal—perhaps a new collar or harness, a crate or cage, a book about the species/breed or general care and training, food samples, or toys.

Some services and supplies will no doubt be donated to your group, but they still have value and should be considered part of the cost of rescuing the animal.

The occasional person may question your adoption fee. After all, these are "unwanted" animals, aren't they? When you prepare your FAQ sheet or web page (*see* Chapter 5), include information on the cost of rescue. Mention the average cost per animal, and perhaps one or two who had extraordinary expenses. Then you will have the numbers at your fingertips when questions come up. Such questions also open the door for talking about the importance of choosing a pet carefully, and then caring for it properly. You can tailor much of that discussion to the specific animals you rescue, but set them in the wider context of pet owning. You can emphasize that the animals in your care are not "unwanted," but in some cases previously wanted for the wrong reasons. (And some, of course, are in rescue due to tragic circumstances.)

I recommend that your volunteers become informed about the current average purchase price of a responsibly bred animal of the species or breed you rescue. Be sure they understand what "responsible" breeding really means in general and in the particular case of "your" animals—quality breeding animals, genetic screening, high-quality pre- and post-natal care, careful evaluation and placement of the babies, and high quality of life for the parents. Being so informed gives everyone a frame of reference and opens the door for educating volunteers and adopters alike about the difference between responsible people who breed for love and improvement of the animals, and pet producers who are in it just for the money. In addition, knowing the "market" will give your volunteers and adopters a firm sense of the great deal that people get when they adopt.

Will a mandatory adoption donation deter adopters? I don't think so. If "how much" is the first question, the person asking is unlikely to be a prime adoption candidate. This is not to say that price isn't an element in the adoption decision, because price is almost always a factor in acquiring an animal, even for serious fanciers. But if price is the *only* hinge on which a person's decision hangs, he is probably not a serious candidate for a rescued animal—or any animal. If raising your adoption fee by fifty dollars makes the difference in whether an adopter can afford to adopt the animal, you need to ask whether the person can afford to maintain the animal or cover occasional emergency expenses. You can always waive or reduce the required donation if you think that's warranted in a special case, but don't haggle with adopters. Doing so demeans your work and the value of the animals you save.

Winston (Winston Thomas CD NJP RAE5 CGC), was rescued by Judy Bireley in 2001 after he was dumped onto a busy highway. Since 2002, Winston has trained at the Fort Wayne (Indiana) Obedience Training Club, and he was the club's first dog to earn the Rally Novice, Rally Advanced, Rally Excellent, Rally Advanced Excellent (RAE), RAE 2, RAE 3, RAE 4, and RAE 5 titles. Winston is also an AKC Canine Good Citizen, and as a certified therapy dog he makes regular visits to nursing homes, often sporting silly outfits to make people smile, and proving that one person's throw-away is another's treasure.
PHOTO BY SHEILA BONEHAM.

SOLICITING SUPPORT

To get money, you have to ask for it. But there's no point asking indiscriminately. You need to put your request before people who are likely to give—people who love animals in general and your kind of animals in particular. Many are "serial donors," giving repeatedly to support the cause, so don't be afraid to approach the same people more than once. Many rescue groups find that some previous adopters continue to contribute on a regular basis in honor of their beloved pets.

Your public library has books and other literature on fund raising, and I recommend you draw on their resources. If you have a volunteer with experience or interest in the field, put her to work finding money—one good fund raiser can make the difference between skimping along from adoption to adoption and having enough financial cushion to support your needs well.

Direct Mail, E-mail, and Newsletters

Rescue groups, like other charities, use many methods to encourage people to donate. Although it is more expensive than some methods, a direct-mail campaign based on a carefully compiled mailing list can bring in donations. Begin with your adopters and volunteers. Ask them to provide the names and addresses of other people who might be interested in your work. Collect names and addresses whenever you participate in special events, and include a sign-up form on your web site for people who want to receive updates on your activities.

For each mailing, compose a letter explaining what your organization is all about, how you are funded ("donations from animal lovers like you"), and what you do with the money you raise. If, like most rescue groups, you are an all-volunteer organization, make that clear. Suggest donation levels to help people decide how much to give. People seem to like names for different levels of contribution, such as "Friend, Best Friend, and Champion," so think about using labels for different donation levels. Offer small, incremental benefits for each level, such as a year's newsletter subscription for Friends, a subscription and t-shirt for Best Friends, or a subscription, t-shirt, and bumper sticker for Champions.

Make it easy for people to donate. If you use e-mail, open an account with PayPal or another reputable service, and include a link in your e-mail. If you use the postal system, include a form that's easy to complete and mail with a check.

Fund Raising Events

Special fund raising events serve two major purposes: they raise funds, and they raise awareness of your rescue program, rescue in general, and the importance of responsible pet ownership and breeding. The possibilities are limited only by the imagination of your volunteers and, in some cases, the space, equipment, or personnel needed for the event. Here are only a few of the many events your group could put on:

- An obedience or agility fun match or Canine Good Citizen (CGC) test open to all breeds of dogs.
- A pet fair with other rescue groups and other groups and businesses that support responsible pet ownership and care.
- A microchip or tattoo clinic.
- A seminar called "So You Want to Breed Your (Dog, Cat, Rabbit)." Recruit an experienced, responsible breeder or two and a veterinarian, and invite the public. Don't preach—detailed, accurate information about the realities and risks of responsible breeding are enough to convince most people that it's not for them. Distribute your literature and ask for donations.
- Pet portraits with Santa Claus, the Easter Bunny, a cartoon character or celebrity, or just by themselves. Recruit a photographer who will donate some or all of the profits.
- A pet-and-owner look-alike contest in conjunction with a community event. Invite the media!
- A silent auction of artwork, books, services, or other items. Have people write down their bids—the highest bidder buys the item. If you have items worth more than a few dollars, specify a minimum starting bid. (Check local auction laws to be sure your event is legal.)
- A raffle. Again, check your state and local laws on gambling and gaming first.
- A garage sale or bake sale.
- A sale of bedding plants in the spring or birdseed in the fall.

Ask for donations of items and services for silent auctions, raffles, and sales, but don't be afraid to pay for attractive prizes. Indiana's Shetland Sheepdog rescue program raffled $100 worth of veterinary services. They issued a check made payable to the veterinarian and mailed it to the winner, and they made several hundred dollars profit. Many pet-supply companies and other businesses are quite generous in exchange for the publicity. A local veterinarian or groomer might donate a service, or an obedience club or trainer might donate partial or full tuition for an obedience course.

Be creative as you look for fund raising possibilities. Team up with people and businesses in ways that benefit you both. Invite an author to give a talk or workshop, sell signed copies of books, and donate a portion of the proceeds to your group. Participate in web site affiliate programs that pay for sales from referrals. Partner with an artist or photographer to promote her work for a commission. Ohio artist Judy Walton, for instance, donates a portion of the sale price from some of her prints to Northern Lights Rescue, and I donate a portion of the price of special prints and commissioned pet portraits, as well as certain book sales, to rescue organizations (visit my web site at www.sheilaboneham.com to learn more, and keep in mind that I love to travel!).

Create a Wish List

If rescue groups had magic lamps, they would want for nothing. Alas, you must create your own light with the help of the many people who are willing to give if they know what is needed. Help your rescue genies by publishing a Wish List in your newsletter and on your web site. Include a copy with your information packets. Indicate which items are on-going needs (litter, bedding, food, cleaning supplies, stamps, prepaid phone or gas cards, and so on) and which are one-time or occasional needs (a new cage or crate, a computer spreadsheet program, and so on).

Ask for More than Money

Cash donations are always welcome, but don't forget that other kinds of donations can save you money and volunteer time. Food, bedding, and equipment for the animals are obvious needs but not always easy for people to get to you. Items like stamps, long-distance phone cards, refills for prepaid cell phones, or gift cards for pet supply stores, gasoline, or other necessities are easy to send and always useful. People may not think of them, though, so include them on your Wish List.

After you clean up the mess and bank the money, be sure to thank your donors and volunteers. It may seem archaic in this electronic age, but a handwritten thank you note goes a long way toward promoting continuing good relations with your supporters.

CUTTING COSTS

The flip side of attracting money is, of course, spending it, which rescue groups do all too well. The biggest expenses for most groups are food, transportation, and veterinary care. Expenditures for equipment, supplies, promotion, and sometimes grooming or other special care also add up quickly. Let's look at some ideas that can help keep costs down.

Minimizing Veterinary Expenses

Veterinary bills are a fact of life for rescue groups, but there are ways to minimize them. Find out if there are reduced-cost spay/neuter programs in your area and whether your group is eligible to use the service (some are earmarked for low-income pet owners). Don't misrepresent your relationship to the animal, but do make it clear that she is under the protection of a rescue organization and that you are an unpaid volunteer. Be sure you know exactly what is covered to avoid nasty surprises—individual vets and clinics vary. We once received some certificates for forty-five dollar spays/twenty-eight dollar neuters, and a list of clinics where they could be used. One clinic charged exactly what the certificate offered. When our volunteer went to pick up a dog from another clinic, though, she was presented with a bill for nearly $200 for add-on "extras" like anesthesia, suturing, and half a day's board during recovery!

Some rescuers seem to think that veterinarians should treat rescued animals free of charge, but such an expectation is unrealistic and unfair. Vets work to make a living, and many already give generously of their time and skills to help shelters, rescue programs, and individual animals in need. On the other hand, there's no reason your volunteers shouldn't ask their own vets to commit to one reduced-cost or even free service per year for a rescue animal. If you have qualified as a 501c corporation for tax purposes, remind your vet that the free service can be written off as a donation. Offer something in return. Acknowledge supportive veterinarians in your newsletter, and offer to include the clinic's business card or brochure in adoption packets. Be sure to provide area veterinarians with information about your group, and to include them on your mailing list. And, of course, patronize contributing vets.

If you live near a veterinary college, ask whether they offer reduced-cost services. One rescuer, for instance, takes her rescued dogs to the teaching hospital of the University of California at Davis Veterinary School, where altering is done at one low cost regardless of complications such as undescended testicles. She writes:

> The surgery is done by a senior vet student under scrupulous supervision by one of the teaching vets, so the safety level is outstanding. The anesthesia and after care (and intensive care if needed) are far superior to that which most vets can provide. The dog's initial exam and history are done by the student and then the supervising vet comes in and double-checks it all. You wind up telling some of the story twice and the dog gets handled a bit more, but from my point of view this is just fine and dandy.

An added benefit is that by using such services, you help raise awareness about rescue and related issues among the veterinarians of the future.

You may be able to save some money on routine procedures, such as basic vaccinations, heartworm tests, and worming, by working with your local shelter. For instance, I arranged to have our local shelter perform heartworm "snap" tests, and to provide most vaccinations at cost (rabies vaccinations must be given by a licensed veterinarian in most places). Because the shelter purchased supplies in large quantities, our rescue organization saved money. Naturally, if you make such an arrangement, you need to offer something in return (*see* Chapter 5 for ideas on working with shelters).

You may also be able to arrange to purchase heartworm preventative, wormers, ear cleansers, flea and tick products, and other supplies at reduced cost through the veterinarians you use. This is another win-win arrangement—you save money on items that you use extensively, and your vets get a little reward for their support.

Donors can help with veterinary expenses, too. Some rescue groups have sponsorship programs whereby an individual pays for some or all of an individual animal's expenses while he is in foster care. One group that I know of established rescue accounts at several area vet clinics, and donors sent money directly to the accounts to be used for rescued animals as needed.

Lowering Expenditures for Food and Supplies

Some rescue programs and their foster caretakers consider the cost of food, litter, and what have you to be part of the volunteer's donation. Other programs provide their foster homes with these daily necessities. Either way, there are some things your organization can do to help control costs for both the group and the volunteers.

Ask the managers of area pet supply stores what they do with packages of food, litter, bedding, shampoo, and other supplies that are damaged and unsalable. Most stores throw them away or donate them to shelters and rescue groups. Ask if you may assign a volunteer to pick up whatever is available on a regular basis. (Be sure the volunteer assigned to this job is reliable, and don't expect stores to keep the supplies for more than a day or so.) Offer to promote the store in return, and follow through.

Let your donors know that you need food from time to time, and offer convenient drop-off spots. Remind donors that they can send you a gift card for a pet supply store and avoid the heavy lifting altogether. Don't make donors work to support your cause—the easier you make it, the more you'll get to help the animals.

Lowering Printing, Advertising, and Mailing Costs

Printing or duplicating informative literature, forms, and contracts can be expensive, but there are ways to cut the costs. To save on copying, printing, advertising, and postage:

- Put your information, application forms, and other written material on your web site, preferably in PDF (Adobe) format to preserve your formatting and to make them easy for people to read and print.
- Ask your volunteers or donors to donate a certain number of copies per month, quarter, or year. Again, prepaid copy accounts or gift cards for copy shops make this easy.
- Ask managers or owners of local copy businesses to donate a certain number of copies in exchange for acknowledgment printed on the copied materials.
- Ask about discounts for prepaying or for purchasing copies in bulk.
- Ask about reduced rates for not-for-profit groups.
- Ask whether rates are lower for certain dates—for instance, it may cost less to advertise in the newspaper on Saturdays than on Sundays.
- Ask about "pay-in-advance" rates—you might be able to run the same ad for consecutive Sundays, for example, for less than if you bought each ad separately.

- Ask people who request information by mail to send stamped, self-addressed envelopes of sufficient size. This weeds out many people who really have no interest after speaking to you but who for some reason are reluctant to say, "No, don't send anything."
- Ask people to send stamps along with their applications to help defray rescue's postage expenses. Most people comply, and many send extra stamps.
- Include postage stamps on your Wish List.
- Post all materials that you mail on your web site for downloading, and give people that option. Many callers will be happy to go to the web site rather than wait for snail mail.

Lust for money may be at the root of some reasons animal rescue groups are needed, but money itself enables us to do the work. May your coffers overflow.

CHAPTER

5

Spreading the Word

To maximize your effectiveness, you have to let people know who you are and what you do. Let's look at some ways to get the word out.

No matter what species or breed of animal we rescue, we all share common challenges, needs, and, for the most part, goals. It makes sense, then, to weave ourselves together into an enormous net to catch animals who need help. And to make this net as wide and strong as possible, we need to include other people who care for the welfare of animals and who behave responsibly, including breeders, exhibitors, and pet owners. We all have things to learn and knowledge to share.

After all, we're presumably all working toward the goal of eliminating the need for rescue except in the most unusual circumstances. When we join forces we can do the improbable, from closing down a puppy mill to fighting bad legislation, from educating buyers about pet stores and why a baby bunny isn't just for Easter to transporting an animal across town or across the country. We support one another, face the inevitable pain of rescue work together, and share the solace of shared experience. Best of all, we celebrate together the many ways in which rescue makes a difference for animals, people, and communities.

NETWORKING ON THE INTERNET

When I wrote Breed Rescue a little more than a decade ago, the potential and power of the Internet were just beginning to be realized. Now it is arguably the most important networking tool available to rescuers. E-mail discussion lists and bulletin boards, web sites and blogs ("web logs," or web-based journals), news groups, and direct e-mail distribution are all used to great advantage by rescue groups and individual rescuers. (See also "Points of Contact" in Chapter 1.)

At its best, on-line communication facilitates rapid and far-flung distribution of information. It creates ties between people who may never meet, and who wouldn't even know of each other's existence if not for web sites and e-mail.

As recent news stories about on-line bullying have emphasized, the Internet also has a destructive side, and it can emerge all too easily in the emotional context of animal rescue. Remind your volunteers to verify all information they obtain on line or off, and to refrain from attacking other people or passing on rumors. On-line attacks rarely accomplish anything positive, and false accusations are almost impossible for innocent people to fight in that environment. A rescuer's time is better spent on positive pursuits.

NETWORKING FACE TO FACE

As I have said elsewhere, rescue work is not just about animals. It's also about people, and the most effective rescuers cooperate with a variety of people, even when they don't all see eye to eye on specific issues.

You can make your initial contacts with many groups through the Internet, but try to meet people in person whenever possible. Events designed to promote rescue and other aspects of responsible pet ownership are natural environments for mingling, but casual encounters can also help build your rescue network. Always carry business cards and, if possible, informational materials that you can hand out whenever opportunity wags its tail at you. If you don't have materials with you, or if you "meet" someone on the phone or online, follow up by mailing her your basic informational packet. (Mark the envelope "Material you requested," so she doesn't think it's just more junk mail.)

The best way to solicit help and cooperation from other people and groups is to help and cooperate with them. This applies whether you're dealing with a shelter, another rescue group, or another type of organization altogether. By giving as well as taking, your group will become known to a wide network of people, will build credibility and good will, and, in the long run, will be able to help more animals. Three types of groups are particularly significant to your basic work: shelters, other rescue groups, and animal-centered organizations. Here are some ideas for building mutually beneficial relationships with each of them.

Shelters

Good working relationships between animal rescue groups and animal shelters benefit everyone. Rescuers offer breed- or species-specific expertise that shelter staff may lack. Shelters harbor animals that have not found their way to a specialized rescue program. And, of course, the animals released to rescue programs benefit directly from individualized care, while other animals gain critical time as space opens up in the shelter.

Over the past decade, more and more shelters have come to recognize the value of rescue groups. But not all shelter personnel like to work with rescue programs, and sometimes they have good reasons. Most rescue organizations and personnel are responsible, realistic, and reliable; some are not. It seems pretty basic, but the best way to combat the negative effects of difficult rescuers and poorly run rescue programs is to treat other people as you like to be treated—by being reliable, trustworthy, and punctual.

Shelters vary not only in their attitudes, but in their organization, funding, staffing, usage, and other factors. Some are part of local or state government agencies. Some are privately funded and run, and some are membership organizations. Their official and de facto policies on euthanasia, release of animals, holding time, and other matters vary wildly. Shelter personnel range from highly knowledgeable and willing to learn to thoroughly and willfully ignorant about the animals in their care and the issues surrounding them. Regardless of the climate of your local shelters, always remember that persistence and example may get through to even the most resistant shelter personnel. Some relationships are built one thin layer of trust at a time.

As you work with shelters, you may have to modify your procedures in some cases, but don't compromise your own ethics. A solid working relationship is built on honesty and reliability. If you take an animal from a shelter on behalf of your group, make it clear that you intend to foster and rehome the animal. Make sure that you have complete ownership and decision-making rights over the animal (*see* "Release of Ownership or Custody" under "Legal Documents" in Chapter 1). Provide copies of your adoption requirements and contracts, and emphasize that all animals you place are spayed or castrated (highlight the spay/neuter clause on your contract). If the person in charge at the shelter won't work with you, see if you can address a meeting of the shelter's governing board. Tell them what your group can do for the shelter, and what the shelter can do for you in return.

Don't lie to save one animal, and be honest about what you can and cannot do. If you simply don't have an available foster home, say so. Don't string shelter staff along. Being anything but honest will damage or destroy any relationship your group has with the shelter, and, because word does get around, it will damage your reputation with other shelters and rescuers. It will also hurt rescue groups in general. Here are some things you might offer to do for the shelter:

- Help identify specific breeds and notify other rescue programs.
- Counsel owners or adopters of your chosen breed or species regardless of where they got their pets.

- Teach shelter staff to identify and distinguish specific breeds through workshops, classes, or one-on-one interaction.

In return, you might ask the shelter to do the following for your group:

- Waive or reduce the standard release fee.
- Provide the standard benefits covered by the fee (especially if you pay the full amount)—this usually includes altering and some veterinary care.
- Provide certain services at cost, such as heartworm tests, inoculations, and worming.
- Provide occasional emergency overnight isolation boarding.
- Provide occasional euthanasia at cost.

It's easy to become frustrated with shelter staff who call you for a misidentified animal, or don't call you for one you would obviously be interested in fostering. Have some empathy. (And honestly, can you identify all breeds of dogs, cats, rabbits, and other sheltered animals?) Shelter personnel are usually overworked, underfunded, and underpaid. They work with frightened, sick, and injured animals, and have to deal with people who frighten, neglect, and hurt animals. They are often in the terrible position of loving animals and having to euthanize hundreds of them. Our job as rescuers is to make their work easier and more effective, so be kind and use the opportunity to educate and help.

Other Rescue Groups

Cooperation among rescue groups does nothing but good for everyone. Particularly within species, rescue groups can help one another in many ways. Even across species, though, we're all striving for essentially the same goals—to eliminate the suffering of pet animals and to place them in proper homes. Educating people about how to choose pets wisely, acquire them responsibly, and care for them properly benefits all animals in the long run.

What can you do to help one another? Here are a few things:

- Locate and identify animals who need help, whether in shelters and other environments, and notify appropriate rescue groups.
- Transport rescued animals for one another when appropriate.
- Split bulk purchases of some supplies.
- Learn from one another's experience.
- Share one another's educational and legal documents.
- Assist with home checks on adopters and foster caretakers.
- Refer potential adopters to one another, especially when your species or breed may not be the best choice for a particular person or family.
- Band together for special events aimed at public education and rescue awareness, such as: a "pet fair"; obedience, rally, or agility fun matches; cat or rabbit agility demos or competitions; a "pet and owner look-alike contest"; a lecture or clinic by a trainer or behaviorist.

People have a natural inclination to become territorial, but it's important to remind ourselves that rescue groups are not in competition with one another. Every successful adoption is a success story that all rescues share.

Other Organizations

Good relations with animal-centered organizations, such as those for fanciers, breeders, and sports enthusiasts, can benefit your rescue group in many ways. Although there are still those who think the need for rescue has nothing to do with them, most serious fanciers know that animals from all backgrounds sometimes find themselves in need. Cultivating their goodwill and support can pay off for your group in ways ranging from financial and material support to hands-on help with animals and events to referrals of potential adopters or volunteers. Make your group known to people and organizations that are in a position to inform the public about your group, including veterinarians, shelters, other rescue groups, obedience schools, animal-oriented clubs, groomers, pet supply stores, and boarding kennels.

If your program is part of a breed club or other group of fanciers, you are subject to the rules and procedures of the club, and you probably depend on it for some or all of your financial support. You obviously already have some level of support from the organization itself and from many individual members, although that can range from generous material and hands-on help to politically correct lip service and little more. A few people might just as soon forget that rescue exists and some may actively oppose allocating resources to your cause. Don't waste your time debating with them. The best argument you can mount for continued support is an effective rescue effort that makes a difference for the animals and people you serve and that promotes responsible breeding, acquisition, and ownership of animals.

Don't underestimate the value of reaching across species lines to educate people and solicit support. Most people who love animals love all kinds of animals, but many are not as well informed as they could be. It can't hurt to publicize your feline or pot-bellied pig rescue program through local dog obedience clubs and vice versa; the benefits to your group and to the animals you help could be tremendous. At the very least you raise awareness, and you may gain financial support, volunteers, and potential adopters.

Hand out brochures and/or business cards. If possible, give appropriate people in businesses and organizations an information packet that includes your mission statement, information about the animals you rescue, requirements for adopters, information for potential volunteers, and anything else you think essential. If you can, assign one volunteer to be a liaison to businesses and other groups. The human face or voice of your group is harder to forget than a brochure among piles of junk mail.

Reach beyond pet-centered groups. Many community groups welcome offers for speakers or programs for their meetings, and many will publish short articles in their newsletters. If an animal or two can accompany you, all the better. Reach out with letters or phone calls, and suggest a few subjects you might talk about for twenty minutes. Solve a problem if possible—how to choose a family pet for the local parents' group, or how to prevent common feline behavior problems. Take your literature along, and perhaps a donation box. Ask your volunteers and adopters to present information to clubs in which they are involved.

Here are some ideas that may help promote your group and build strong, supportive bonds with other groups:

- Ask for space in the newsletter for rescue-related stories.
- Ask for space to set up an information booth or put out literature at the organization's meetings or other events.
- Offer to help with the club's events—most groups need people to help set up, clean up, and do all sorts of other jobs. Dog sports clubs in particular always need people for everything from pooper scoopers to ring stewards to scorekeepers. If a few of your volunteers can help another group, you create good will, and that can't help but benefit rescue and the animals.

PUBLICITY AND THE MEDIA

We live in the age of electronics, and rescue groups can tap the potential of various media to solicit support, recruit volunteers, attract adopters, locate needy animals, and educate people about animals. Regardless of whether you utilize print media (mainly newspapers, newsletters, and magazines), the Internet, radio, or television, there are two main avenues: advertising and publicity.

Many rescue groups advertise in newspapers, magazines, and newsletters, often generating a lot of interest. Small classified ads are often inexpensive, but advertising costs can climb quickly. Publicity, on the other hand, can generate considerable interest for the low cost of getting your message to the media. The trick is to make your message one that the recipients will pass along.

Media outlets receive much more information than they can use, so they obviously select what they perceive as the most relevant and interesting for their audience and the most in line with their purpose. Your job is to get the media excited about your message. Here are some suggestions:

- Don't rely solely on other people's newsletters. Start your own. Distribute it by mail and/or e-mail, and post it on your web site. Your newsletter can be used to keep volunteers, adopters, donors, and other interested parties up to date on your activities and needs, and the animals in your care.
- Find an angle that makes your message stand out and shows media decision-makers that your story offers news, entertainment, or information that will appeal

Australian Shepherd Reno and his sister Jasmine were poster children for the role good breeders can play in pet rescue. Responsibly bred, the pups were sold to a buyer in another state as show prospects. The breeder's trust turned out to be misplaced, but getting the dogs away from the buyer proved difficult. In the end, using the buyer's failure to make payments as legal leverage, the pups' breeder called on fellow breeder Heidi Mobley and the local sheriff to repossess the dogs. Jasmine was physically and mentally crippled and had to be euthanized. Reno was emaciated, and his fur was matted to the skin and bleached out from unsheltered exposure. Another breeder, Shelly Seybold, took Reno in and began his long rehabilitation. From there he came to the author's home, where he blossomed (see perennialaussies.com/reno.html). Despite the abuse and neglect he experienced, Reno loved people and other animals. I never once heard him growl. He was an outstanding therapy dog, particularly with autistic children, and I imagine him even now surrounded by kids who need him. PHOTO BY SHEILA BONEHAM.

to their audience. There's nothing revolutionary about people taking in homeless animals and finding them new homes. But how many people realize that there are rescue groups devoted to all breeds of dogs? How many know about cat rescue groups, or rabbit or rat or pot-bellied pig rescue groups? How many know that adult animals will indeed bond with new owners and suit many people better than a baby animal would?

- Show how your group, or a specific service or event, benefits the community in unique ways. What's new or different about your service (or product or event)? How is it distinct from other services in the broad field of humane assistance?

What problem does your rescue service address, and how does it do so? How effective is it?

- Appeal to human interest. Has one of your rescued dogs become a search-and-rescue dog or achieved a high-level performance title? Does one of your rescued cats or bunnies visit a local nursing home? Has a celebrity adopted a pet from your group? Such stories have tremendous audience appeal.

Generate Interest

One person in your group should serve as your group's publicist and be responsible for establishing and maintaining relations with the news media and for sending media releases to news directors, reporters, columnists, producers, community-affairs directors, talk-show hosts, and other appropriate people.

A *media release* is a short notice designed to alert media outlets to news or an event of interest. The person who receives *your* release probably receives hundreds of releases a week, so it's a good idea to follow a fairly standard format that makes information easily accessible. The details of preparing media releases and other publicity materials are beyond the scope of this book, but many books and web sites explain how to do it effectively.

Who should receive your media releases? That will depend on your community and the particular announcement, but some possibilities include:

- News editors of daily and weekly newspapers and specialized local pet tabloids.
- News editors at area radio, television, and cable news stations.
- Feature editors of daily and weekly newspapers.
- Consumer-interest and feature reporters.
- Radio and television program producers.
- Photo editors for local newspapers.
- Editors of city or regional magazines.

Have your publicist prepare a *media kit*, a set of materials that provide background information about your group. Here are some things you might include:

- List of officers, board members, and other key volunteers, and their contact information.
- Brochure or general information sheet.
- Adoption guidelines.
- Description of the breed or type of animal you rescue.
- Testimonials (a single page of quotations from adopters and others who have worked with your group is plenty).
- A list of Frequently Asked Questions (FAQs) and their answers—keep it to one sheet, front and back.

- Copies of previous print media coverage.
- List of previous radio and television coverage.

If your budget allows, include one or more high-quality 5 x 7 or 8 x 10-inch photos. They should be appealing, in focus, and have backgrounds that don't obscure or distract from the animals or people they show. At least one should be in color. Attach a typed or printed label to the back of each photo to identify the subject(s) and the photographer. *Don't write on the photo itself, either front or back.* On a standard sheet of paper, write additional information about each photo, making sure that the photo to which it pertains is clear. If you put media information on your web site, provide a link to download high-resolution photos suitable for printing or to contact someone who can send them.

Put everything together in a folder, with the information about current news in the right-hand pocket, and general background information in the left. Label the outside of the folder, and include the name, phone number, and e-mail address of your contact person. Send the kit to editors, reporters, and producers who express interest in your group or activities. Clip a cover letter to the outside of the folder, and address it to a specific person (not "Dear Editor," "Dear Reporter," and *definitely* not "Dear Sir"). If someone has requested information, you have a name. If not, call ahead—a telephone receptionist can give you the information. The letter should be very brief—"I'm sending you our media kit for your information and use." Let the kit speak for itself. You may want to put a media page with the same materials on your web site—be sure it's in an easy-to-print form, such as PDF.

ADDITIONAL IDEAS FOR PUBLICITY

Look for other creative ways to generate publicity and to educate people about their pets. Here are a few ideas.

Proclamations

Ask your mayor, city council, board of education, a local civic organization, or even a neighborhood association to issue an official proclamation or pass a resolution in recognition of a special event or issue. For instance, ask the mayor of your town to make a certain week Canine Training Week to promote responsible dog ownership, or ask local schools to proclaim the month before Easter "Rabbit Responsibility Month" to curtail impulse bunny buying.

Events

Band together with other rescue organizations, shelters, trainers, or other groups for a "Pet Lovers Day." Set up displays, distribute information, and offer demonstrations,

competitions and contests, or the AKC's Canine Good Citizen Test. Sponsor Kids &
Pets Safety Week, complete with visits to schools and libraries to teach children how
to interact safely and kindly with animals. Notify the media.

You may be able to get double publicity out of an event if you send a follow-up
release. Include fresh "new news" to interest the media in the second release. For instance, if you ran a contest or competition, you can announce the winners. Include a
photograph if possible.

Community Calendars

Many newspapers, radio and television stations, cable channels, and on-line resources
offer free community calendar listings for local events. Many public libraries and local
businesses offer bulletin boards for publicizing local events, and many have display
cases available for individuals and community groups. These are useful even without
any event to publicize, because pictures of animals invariably attract attention.

TEACHING MORE THAN RESCUE

Public appearances and promotional materials from rescue groups should, naturally,
spread the word about the animals in need of help and homes, and how rescue groups
work on their behalf. Beyond that, rescuers should make information available to help
people make good choices about pets and to give them the tools they need to make
rescue work unnecessary.

How much your group can do depends on how many volunteers you have, how
much time they can contribute, where you are located, what resources you have available, and other factors. Here are some ideas:

- Set up information kiosks or tables at shopping malls, pet shows, community
  events, and other public places. Use photos of rescued animals to attract attention. Think creatively—set up a cat or rabbit rescue display at a dog show, or a canine rescue display at a home and garden show.
- Offer literature if possible—many pet food and equipment manufacturers, registries and clubs, veterinary clinics and associations, and other sources offer free
  literature on just about every topic you can imagine. (Read everything first,
  though, to be sure you agree with the content. You don't want to inadvertently
  promote a training method or political agenda you oppose.)
- Team up with other rescue groups, and support responsible breeding. Why not
  hand out material on how to choose a reputable breeder? Why not exchange material with other rescue programs to promote one another? If you don't think that
  the animals you rescue are quite right for a certain person, why not encourage
  him to look into more appropriate breeds, or even a different species? Anything

that will encourage people to obtain and keep their pets responsibly will help *all* rescue efforts and, most importantly, all animals.

- Strike at the source of some of the problem—backyard or casual pet production—through innovative approaches. Hand out literature on ethical breeding practices and the hazards of letting Lady or Puff have "just one litter." Many people are so focused on the idea of having cute puppies or kittens, or the possibility of making a little money, that they don't think about the down side of breeding, including the risk to the mother's life. And, with puppies especially, don't forget to mention the poop!

Information is a powerful tool, and although it sometimes seems that no one is listening, you will reach some people.

Rabbits and other small pets often suffer when people buy them on impulse or as gifts for children without considering the needs of the animals. All rescuers and responsible pet owners can help reduce the number of relinquished and neglected small pets by becoming educated, passing on information, and setting an example for other people, no matter what kind of pets we choose. PHOTO BY ERIC ISSELÉE.

DELAYED REACTIONS

Don't be too disappointed if nothing happens immediately after you start a publicity campaign. People file away the information to use later themselves, or to hand on to someone else. When we set up our first library display, it didn't seem to have any effect until someone finally called three months later, but within six months we had a new volunteer, two successful adoptions, another adoption application, and had referred one person to another breed rescue program and one to a reputable breeder. They had all seen the display and picked up brochures. It is said that people have to see something three times before they notice it. Keep your information out there and sooner or later you'll see results.

PART

2

The
Animals

CHAPTER

6

Animals In Need, or What It's All About

Animals need rescuing for reasons that run the gamut from reasonable to tragic to foolish to criminal. Some people relinquish their pets directly to rescue programs or to animal shelters that in turn release them to rescuers. Stray animals may enter rescue programs right off the street, or by way of a shelter or Good Samaritan. Some animals come to rescue after being legally seized because they have been abused or neglected. Each of these sources presents different practical, legal, and ethical challenges for rescuers.

We begin this chapter with suggestions that apply to most, if not all, rescued animals, and then move to animals from specific sources. (*See also* Chapter 1 on "Establishing Policies and Procedures.")

ANIMAL MANAGEMENT BASICS

Some of the animals you handle will arrive in good condition, with veterinary and other written information that vouches for their health and social skills. For many, though, you will have no background information about past veterinary care, possible exposure to disease and parasites, training, or behavioral quirks. You'll be able to make educated guesses about some of these critical factors, but others are invisible or slow to surface.

It can be tempting when faced with an animal in dire straights to ignore caution and just scoop him up and take him home. I won't say that's never appropriate—I've done it myself. But handling animals whose histories are unknown does pose hazards, and given a choice, I encourage you always to opt for the safest possible procedures. Your own safety, and the health and safety of your human, animal, and rescue families, must always come first.

Safety and Disease Prevention

Dealing with living creatures always carries potential risks. As a rescuer, you'll find that most animals are astonishingly trusting and willing to accept our help. Others are too frightened or confused to let down their guard, and some are aggressive. Even when the animal's behavior poses no danger, he may carry disease or parasitic organisms that threaten other animals and, occasionally, people.

Here are some suggestions to facilitate easier, safer handling:

- Don't take foolish risks. You don't want the animal to panic and hurt himself, and you don't want him to hurt you or anyone else. Trust me, being bitten or clawed hurts like crazy, and an animal does not have to be very large to inflict serious, permanent damage. Being bitten is the one animal experience I could have lived without. (*See also* Chapters 2, 8, and 9 on inter-animal safety.) The following procedures will reduce the risk of mishap: If the animal is wearing a flat or buckle collar that is easy to slip, or no collar, improvise a slip collar or a harness with a leash, rope, or belt. A slip collar or harness is difficult for an animal to duck out of and gives you more control.
- Use a leash (or makeshift version)—don't try to guide an unfamiliar animal with your hands.
- Don't pick the animal up unless he is very small and quiet, and then do so carefully, and be prepared to put him down if he panics.
- Don't put your face within striking distance.
- Don't reach for an animal that growls, bares teeth, hisses, swats, or otherwise warns you off. If he threatens to hurt you, believe him. Find a safer means of control or wait for help.

With an animal whose medical history is unknown, there is also a risk of disease. The animal's appearance will give you some idea of his health, but not always (*see* Chapters 2, 3, and 8 on health and safety precautions).

Transporting a Rescued Animal

The need to move animals from place to place is a given of rescue work. Although people do drive many miles with animals loose in their vehicles, it's not a good idea.

No one needs a frightened, agitated, or rambunctious animal bouncing around the car, leaping onto the driver's lap (or head), or crawling under seats and around pedals.

If the animal has fleas or other parasites and travels loose, he'll no doubt leave unwelcome critters on the carpets and upholstery for the next passenger to pick up. If he's nervous or not used to riding in a car, he may vomit, defecate, or urinate. And if you have the misfortune to be in an accident, he is at risk of injury or escape. Most animals can be transported more safely in crates, which:

- Keep them from roaming or being thrown around the vehicle.
- Limit or prevent physical contact with vehicle surfaces, allowing for more effective cleaning and disinfecting.
- Confine most or all fleas and other parasites (and their larvae and eggs).
- Confine bodily fluids if the animal becomes ill or needs to relieve himself.
- Restrain and protect the animals in an accident.
- Separate animals if you are transporting more than one.

The safest crates are those approved for airline transport. Plastic airline crates are relatively inexpensive, and come in sizes suited for animals ranging from tiny to two hundred pounds. They are lighter weight than metal crates, which can be important if you rescue medium to large animals, and they are easy to clean and disinfect.

Metal crates are also good, but have a few drawbacks. They are heavier than plastic, which makes the larger ones hard to manage, and because the sides are spaced wire, they don't keep the surrounding area as clean as closed plastic crates do.

Two other options are available but not well suited to rescue work. Lightweight crates made of fabric stretched on collapsible frames have become popular with dog owners over the past few years, but they are easy to escape, and they are so light weight that an active animal can move or roll them. Disposable crates or carriers made of cardboard are also available and work with some cats and small animals. However, an agitated or persistent creature can claw and chew his way out.

In a pinch, you can tie the animal, preferably in the back, away from the driver. Use a harness, not a collar, and cross tie the animal—that is, use two leashes or ropes, fastening one to one side of the vehicle and one to the other side with enough slack to allow some movement while limiting the animal's range.

What if someone is available to hold the animal? Again, that's not the best option, but may be necessary in an emergency. If possible, wrap the animal in a towel or blanket to restrain him and prevent possible bites or scratches if he becomes frightened.

Who Are You? Checking for Identification

Unless an animal is handed over by his owner, one of the first things you need to do is check him for identification. In fact, I recommend that even owner-relinquished animals be checked for permanent identification to be sure the animal has not been reported missing by a third party, and to transfer the contact information to your group. It may be, too, that the breeder registered the animal with a microchip or tattoo registry that the owner neglected to mention (*see* "Who You Gonna Call" later in this chapter).

Here are the steps to locating and using identification, if present:

- Tags: If the animal is not an owner turn-in and is wearing a collar, check for tags. Even if there is no up-to-date name tag, you may be able to trace the owner through a city or county license number, or through the veterinarian who issued the rabies tag.
- Microchips: Have the animal scanned for the presence of a microchip. If your group does not have a scanner, an area animal shelter, veterinarian, or other rescue group may let you use theirs. Check over the animal's shoulders and down the back and sides. If a number appears, write it down, and contact the registries to find out who registered the animal.
- Tattoos: Tattoos are not as common as they were before the era of microchips, but some people still tattoo their pets, usually on the belly or inner thigh. If the animal is hairy or has dark skin, the tattoo may be hard to see. If you find a tattoo, check with the registries.

Microchip and Tattoo Registries

- PETtrac/AVID Microchips, 800-336-2843, www.avidmicrochip.com/pet-trac.htm
- HomeAgain MicroChips/Companion Animal Recovery, 800-252-7894, 5580 Centerview Drive, Suite 250, Raleigh, NC 27606-3394, www.akc.org/love/car
- Tatoo-A-Pet, 800-828-8667, 1625 Emmons Avenue, Brooklyn, NY 11235, www.tattoo-a-pet.com
- National Dog Registry, 800-NDR-DOGS, www.natldogregistry.com

PHONE CALLS AND PAPERWORK

Background Information

When you talk to people who want to relinquish pets to you, or have you refer potential adopters to them, don't assume anything! Ask specific questions, preferably in person or by telephone. If you have the relinquishing owner fill out a written form, confirm the answers in a face-to-face interview if possible, so you can observe not only what the person says, but how he says it. Use written answers by themselves only as a last resort.

I got a call one evening from a friend who said I needed to come see what followed her home. That's when I met Malcolm, a half-grown red tabby who had linked up with Alice and her two dogs on their walk, although she tried to tell him she didn't need another cat. The little guy was bold as brass and went home with me, where he quickly became my constant companion and best buddies with my Lab, Raja. No one ever responded to the ads or flyers we posted, and Malcolm was home to stay.
Photo by Sheila Boneham.

It is very common for people to omit information or lie outright about the pets they relinquish, and the "reason" many people give is often not the real reason they are giving up the pet. Ask about specific behaviors or health issues that are common in the animals you rescue (*see* Chapters 8 and 9). Here are some queries to get you started:

- Has this animal ever bitten or tried to bite a person? If so, what were the circumstances?
- Has this animal ever bitten, attacked, or tried to bite or attack another animal? If so, what kind of animal and under what circumstances?
- Is this animal potty trained?
- How does this animal react to children? Other animals?

- Does this animal have any unusual behaviors? (I once fostered a dog who barked non-stop except when he was in a car.)
- If you were to keep this animal, what one or two things would you change about him or her?
- Has this animal ever had (choose as appropriate for your type of animal), for instance, a seizure, chronic lameness, skin problem?

Relinquishment Forms

When you take an animal from the owner, the owner and a representative of your group should sign a written form that:

- Confirms that the person signing is the animal's sole legal owner or is acting at the owner's behest.
- Provides a complete description of the animal (attach photos from the front and both sides if possible).
- Provides the name and contact information for the breeder, shelter, or rescue group from which the animal was obtained, if known.
- Provides the name and contact information for the animal's veterinarian (attach records if available).
- Transfers registration of any permanent identification (microchip or tattoo) the animal has.
- Transfers ownership of the animal to your rescue group, including all further claims to and interest in the animal.

Owners Who Won't Let Go

Some rescue calls remain with you for years. I remember one from 1994. It was Thursday, and the woman who called had to get the young male Lab out of her home before the following Monday (when the new carpet would be installed), and wanted rescue to take him, care for him, and find him a new home. But she also wanted to interview and approve the adopter, and have visiting rights while he was in foster care and after he was adopted. We declined. *Be cautious* about taking an animal with conditions attached. As an alternative, offer suggestions (possibly a handout) to help the person rehome the animal responsibly. (Referrals are an option, but consult an attorney first, because you cannot vouch for animals not in your care). The end of the story? The woman called back Saturday evening, frantic, and signed the dog over to our rescue program on Sunday, no strings attached. He went to a home where he was more important than the carpet.

Who You Gonna Call?

Many people relinquish their pets with no paperwork and little information, but some people provide all sorts of records. Be sure to ask for whatever is available—people don't always realize how useful the information is to rescuers and adopters. If you get paperwork, have a volunteer follow up on the information (this is a great job for someone who wants to help without handling the animals).

Contact the animal's breeder. I can tell you from experience that it is devastating for a responsible breeder to wonder what became of a puppy or kitten or other animal entrusted to a buyer. (I have been searching for two of my puppies for several years—read about them at perennialaussies.com, and if you know these dogs, please tell me.) Many ethical breeders will take the animal to keep or rehome (been there, done both), or will underwrite the expenses of fostering the animal, and they should be given that opportunity. People are often too embarrassed to tell the breeder they can't keep the pet, or are just too lazy to be bothered. Contact the breeder even if the owner says he already did. If you don't tell the breeder, she may never know that the animal has lost his home.

Keeping Records

Your rescue program should set up a good system for keeping records on all the animals you handle. Good records will help you understand where your animals and adopters come from, where your money comes from and goes, what individual volunteers do for the effort, and so on.

Computers make record keeping easier and less ponderous than a paper file system, although you won't be able to eliminate paper altogether. Many basic spread sheets are simple to learn, set up, and maintain, and most word processing programs allow you to create standard forms that you can print as needed. Just be sure to back up all computer files onto CDs or travel drives at least once a week.

Each animal you take in should have an individual record that includes the following:

- Name and contact information for the person or organization who released the animal to you.
- For strays, when and where the animal was found, how he was caught, and his condition at that time. If possible, attach a photo taken when you acquired the animal, especially if he is dirty, injured, or thin.
- If the animal was not turned in by his owner, what, if any, identification you found on him, and what attempts you made to locate his owner.
- What expenditures you made on the animal's behalf.
- Where the animal was fostered.
- What happened to the animal.

The devil, as they say, is in the details, and having good records can save you a lot of trouble in some situations. Suppose the owner contacts you after you have placed the animal in an adoptive home. Good records can protect you from accusations of theft and from liability for damages if you had the animal spayed or neutered or otherwise "damaged." Records also legitimize your standing as a not-for-profit organization.

POINTS OF ORIGIN

As we've seen, animals come into rescue programs from many places and for many reasons. Let's take a more detailed look at the most common.

Straight from the Owner

People give up pets for many reasons. Too many rescuers are quick to condemn people out of hand for making an often heart-wrenching decision not to keep an animal. Please don't do that. Granted, you'll run into some criminally stupid and irresponsible people if you're in rescue for very long, but every case should be evaluated on its own merits.

When you deal with owners who want to relinquish their pets, keep in mind that they do have at least a smidgen of concern for the animal (and often much more than a smidgen). Yes, they're asking you to assume a responsibility they took on themselves. But consider the many other "solutions" that are available, and at least give people credit for choosing rescue. The fact is that sometimes *not* keeping a pet is the most responsible thing that a person can do. Forever in the wrong home isn't good for anyone, least of all the animal.

So why do people give pets to rescue programs? Some people die, leaving one or more pets behind, and family members and friends are not always in a position to keep the animals. For others, illness or other life-altering problems make it impossible to care properly for a pet. Profound changes in a person's income, job responsibilities, or other elements of daily life sometimes make responsible pet care impossible or impractical.

Inexperienced owners can be overwhelmed by the reality of owning a pet, or a particular pet. It may be that a person failed to do his homework before getting the animal, but it may also be that he tried but was misinformed. Rescuers can perform "interventions" in some of these cases to help people figure out a solution that lets them keep their pets (*see* Chapter 7). At other times, the best thing for the pets as well as the people involved may in fact be to move the animal to a more appropriate home or, in extreme cases involving aggression or serious illness, to have the animal euthanized.

Even a responsible pet owner can find that an individual animal just isn't working out and needs to be in a different home. I confess, I'm a bit mystified by the shock some people express at this idea. We don't bond with every human being we meet (or live with), so why should we expect to bond with every member of another species? Even within a litter, individual personalities can vary radically, and one person's ideal pet may be too quiet, too exuberant, too soft, too dominant, too clingy, or too independent for another person. And vice versa—a pet that merely gets by in one home may blossom in another. This is why careful placements are vital, and why rescuers can sometimes help fix a mismatch.

You will run into some owners whose reasons and actions are offensive and stupid. The ones who bought the Irish Wolfhound and then underfed him so he wouldn't grow too big (he did anyway—my parents adopted him when I was in high school). The ones who got the Siamese kitten and are annoyed that he "talks" all the time. The ones who didn't get the girl spayed and are appalled that she "got herself" pregnant.

The temptation to slap someone silly can make your fingers tingle. Don't. No tongue lashing, either. Be civil and business-like with everyone, for your own sake and that of the animal. If you get nasty, the owner may walk away. What then of the animal he wants to give up? Besides, you may be able to chip away at ignorance, especially if you're facing an obvious case of "wrong pet" syndrome. For many people, handing a pet over to rescue is very difficult. Most people have developed some emotional attachment to their pets even if they know they can't or shouldn't keep them. Most experience a wild mix of sadness, relief, regret, guilt, embarrassment, and loss. Why rub it in? Use the opportunity to educate. Compassion for people as well as animals will accomplish far more than nastiness, and you will feel better for being civil and kind.

When you accept an animal from the owner, follow the procedures established by your governing board (*see* Chapter 1). If the owner has registration papers, try to have them signed over to you. Some registries do not allow an organization to be the registered owner, so a rescue representative will have to act as designated owner. Sometimes the *legal* owner is not the *registered* owner. Many people never send in the registration paperwork they receive with their pets, and if the registered owner has died, the person relinquishing the pet to you is probably not on the registration. In such a case, take the papers anyway if possible. Otherwise, ask for a photocopy, or write down the name and address of the owner of record, the breeder, the animal's date of birth, and, if you don't already have the information, the registry.

Animals from Shelters and Other Rescue Programs

In Chapter 5, we explored the ins and outs of working with animal shelters; now we'll look at the animals who come from the shelters. They run the full gamut from show-quality purebreds to mystery mixes. Animals picked up as strays or dumped anonymously at the shelter arrive, of course, with no background information, as do some pets turned in by their owners or agents of the owners. A small minority arrive with background information and written records.

Occasionally a rescue program takes in an animal that isn't the kind they normally handle, and then transfers the animal to a more appropriate group. This is especially true for rare breeds, for which rescue options may be few and far between. Many of the same principles apply when you take animals from both shelters and other rescuers.

It is not uncommon for owners to omit information, or lie outright, about the animal's history and behavior, particularly if the animal has a history of biting. Many behavioral and health issues that may impel someone to take an animal to a shelter won't be obvious in the shelter environment, or even in early days of foster care, but may reappear later. (*See* "Background Information" (page 66) and "Straight from the Owner"(page 70) for a summary of the kinds of information you may need to ascertain by trial and error.)

One big reason to transfer animals from shelters to rescue-group foster homes when possible is to facilitate accurate assessment of their personalities and behavior. Many animals are frightened in a shelter environment, and do not show well as adoption candidates. Stressed animals often do things they would not do in normal circumstances, and the behavior they exhibit in a shelter may not be typical. Wait until the animal has settled into a foster home before you attempt a serious assessment (other than obvious signs of aggression that could endanger someone or someone's pets).

Be sure that the paperwork you sign with the shelter gives you full ownership of the animal and the right to place him in a new home. Don't sign a standard shelter contract that requires you to return the animal rather than rehome him. If possible, have a shelter representative sign a relinquishment form designed by your group and approved by your attorney. Don't lie to save one animal—doing so will come back to haunt you and everyone else doing rescue work. The same applies, of course, if you take an animal from another rescue program. Finally, when you take an animal from a shelter or other rescue group, follow the same intake procedures you use for other animals.

Seized Animals

Animals who have been seized from their owners by civil authorities pose a difficult problem for rescuers. Whether they arrive alone or in appallingly large numbers, they are nearly always seized because they have been abused or neglected. They pull our hearts into raw little knots, and they need enormous investments of time, money, work, and care to be brought back to physical and mental health. Some can't be saved, despite valiant efforts.

Although success stories abound, be realistic and cautious about committing your resources to handle and foster animals that have been forcibly removed from their owners. Request confirmation *in writing* of the legal status of the animals. If your group will not have full legal ownership of the animals, including the right to have them spayed or neutered, to place them in new homes, or to have them euthanized if necessary, then grit your teeth and walk away. Several years ago a shelter where I volunteered took in thirty-seven seized animals, including dogs, cats, horses, and a goat, which they had to house and care for until the court case ended, turning away other animals for lack of space during that time. The owner fought the seizure in court for almost *four years*, and prevailed. They got their animals back.

As much as we would like the authorities to be able to remove animals from wretched conditions, they cannot do so without legal authority, and, as they say, the wheels of justice grind slowly. In the end, the animals seized and rehabilitated may be returned to the owner. Your time, money, energy, foster homes, and emotions may be better spent on public education, and on animals with a better potential future.

Buddy showed up in Joe Murphy's neighborhood on Good Friday 2003 with no collar, no tags, no microchip. Joe thinks he was dumped or abandoned at some nearby apartments. Buddy was gentle and well-behaved, and Joe posted flyers, placed a "found" ad, and called local shelters, but no one claimed Buddy. Joe says, "I promised Buddy that I would take care of him if no one would take him. Needless to say, Buddy has been part of our family ever since." Buddy and Joe have a great time together training and competing in obedience, agility, and tracking, and Buddy's official handle is now Buddy CD, NA, NAJ, UAG1. Buddy is also a gentle therapy dog. As Joe says, "The day Buddy showed up turned out to be a blessing for both of us."

Strays

Rescue groups are often called upon to help with stray animals. Unless someone else has already done so, you have to catch a stray before you can help him. Some animals will come right to you, some will run the other way, and some will perform a combination of approach and avoid behaviors. For a pet, being lost can be very disorienting and frightening, and even animals that are usually friendly and confident may be cautious and jittery. If the animal is ill or injured to boot, his behavior is even more unpredictable.

The watchword, then, is caution. Even if the animal appears to be friendly, proceed slowly, gently, and carefully. Encourage all of your volunteers to learn as much as possible about body language as well as safe handling procedures. If you are not confident that you can safely handle or confine an animal, *leave him alone*. Go for help, such as your local shelter or animal control service, or come back later with one or two more people and better equipment.

If you can't approach the animal closely enough to get a leash or blanket on him or to put him into a crate, try a humane trap designed to capture without injury. Some animals are reluctant to enter a confined space, but with enough patience and attractive lures, most can be caught. Many shelters and vets have humane traps available for rent (or free in certain cases), or you can, of course, purchase one if you expect to need it often.

Whatever your feelings about animals, legally they are property, and the law assumes that the owner of lost property wants that property back. Although rescue organizations usually are not governed by the laws that apply to animal shelters, those laws are a reasonable guide for dealing with found animals. Most jurisdictions require that a stray animal be held three to ten days before being destroyed or placed for adoption, unless the animal is seriously ill or injured, or poses a danger to people. After that, the animal is considered to be abandoned property, and the former owner has no further legal claim.

More important, you have an ethical responsibility to both the animal and his owner to try to reunite them. For all you know, the animal may have been stolen or may have gotten lost through no fault of the owner. The owner may be looking for the animal, and the animal for the owner. Here are the most efficient ways to search for a lost owner:

- Check the "lost" ads in your local newspapers.
- Place a "found" ad in your local newspapers (they're often free). Give only enough information to avoid irrelevant calls—species or breed, for instance.
- Check the area where the animal was found for "lost" flyers, and post flyers of your own.
- Post information to relevant e-mail lists and web sites.
- Check with local shelters, veterinarians, dog training facilities, pet supply stores, and other relevant people and businesses, and take them copies of your flyers.

If someone claims the animal, he should be able to identify the animal to your satisfaction. Ideally, he will have photos, veterinary records, and additional paperwork to prove ownership. The animal will probably tell you whether this is his person, but preliminary screening will save you and the person looking for a lost animal a lot of time and disappointment.

If you do find the owner, tell him about your organization and ask to be reimbursed for any money you spent on behalf of his pet. Most people will give that and more in gratitude. Some become long-term supporters of animal rescue.

Wherever they come from and whatever they are, rescued pets have one thing in common: they need homes where they will be cherished, respected, and cared for properly. We'll talk about the rehoming process in Chapter 10. Before we send them into their new lives, though, rescued animals should be screened for health problems (Chapter 8) and for temperament and behavioral issues (Chapter 9). But first, let's see what rescuers can do to keep some animals in their current homes when appropriate.

CHAPTER

7

The Human Side of Rescue Work

Many well-meaning animal lovers are completely in the dark about how to choose the right pet and care for the animal in ways that prevent problems and promote understanding and harmony between species. Furthermore, many people have no idea how to manage problems they encounter as pet owners or where to get help. Although you will probably run into some abusive owners, most people who decide to relinquish pets to rescue groups do not fall under that umbrella. More often, they are frustrated by pet-related problems that they simply don't know how to solve. Rescue volunteers can do at least three important things to improve the situation:

- Educate current and would-be pet owners, and new adopters, and point them toward additional sources of information and assistance.
- Counsel adopters during at least the first few months after the adoption, especially if the adoptee has had health or behavior problems in the past.
- Set an example by being responsible pet owners and by educating ourselves about our own favorite animals and others.

Rescuers and others committed to responsible pet ownership also need to develop empathy and compassion not only for animals, but for people as well. The emotional aspect of rescue work makes it easy to paint with a broad brush, and to disparage anyone who "gets rid of" a pet. I certainly had that attitude when I first became involved with rescue, breeding, competing, and writing about all of the above. But the truth is that we are not privy to people's thoughts and feelings, nor to the details of their lives, and sometimes rehoming a pet is best for both the owner *and the pet.*

When speaking to owners with "problem" pets, guide them toward solutions that will keep the animal in the current home if that seems appropriate and if the owner seems to want to work things out. Keep in mind, though, that the reasons people give for what they (we!) do are not always the real reasons. If a person resists the possibility of keeping the pet, accept that choice and try not to judge.

THE CULTURAL SETTING

Most American pet owners seem to operate by a set of conflicting principles. People "love animals," as long as the animals don't behave too much like, well, animals. People want their dogs to be calm, well-behaved, and self-cleaning, but they don't always train and exercise the dogs to help them be that way. People don't want their cats to rip up the furniture, but they don't provide scratching facilities or trim those kitty cat claws. People want all their pets to be not too messy or noisy or needy. Ironically, many people also have very low expectations for good behavior and health in their pets, and an astonishing cluelessness about why pets do "bad" things.

What Did You Say?

We live in an age of platitudes—stock phrases that seem to have meaning until you look below the surface. Maybe it's my background in linguistics and writing that makes my brain itch when I hear or read them, but please think about what commonly used terms really mean before you use them. Here are some that bug me.

- "Pet Parent" and "Fur Baby"—Cute, but many of the problems that people have with their pets arise from failure to see the animals as *animals.* They are not our children, and we are not their parents. We are their owners, friends, playmates, and protectors, not their mommies and daddies, and we demean them when we fail to recognize and honor them for what they really are.
- "Guardian"—Animal rights groups often advocate for a change in legal terminology that would make those of us with pets their "guardians" rather than their "owners." While that may seem harmless, and even attractive to

those who consider themselves "pet parents," guardianship would be a political and legal nightmare for most of us. It would give pets legal rights and take many decisions concerning them out of our hands, potentially dictating such things as the type and level of veterinary care we must provide, and even the right to make the difficult decision to euthanize a pet suffering from old age or devastating injury or disease. Promote responsible *ownership.*

- "Forever Home"—Although the idea that an animal will stay forever in one home is lovely, this term suggests that a "Not Forever Home" is always bad. If that were true, we would not be able to rescue, foster, and rehome animals. Breeders would not be able to place puppies or kittens or other babies in new homes. Service dog groups could not use puppy raisers, or place trained dogs with people who need them, or rehome dogs that turn out to be unsuited to the work. Pets whose owners die or become unable to care for them would be doomed. There are many good reasons for animals to be rehomed, by rescuers and by breeders and owners, and we should rejoice in the fact that most animals adjust well and learn to love again. The critical question is not whether the animal was rehomed, but whether he was moved from his previous home responsibly.

An appalling number of pets are victims of neglect, although their owners would be shocked to hear me say that their pampered pets are neglected. But the fact is that many well-meaning people create problems by failing to give their pets the basic tools of good behavior and optimum health: physical exercise, mental stimulation, proper nutrition, regular grooming, and basic training. Many people—even those who have had pets all of their lives—lack the most basic knowledge about their own pets and their needs. More important, many people don't realize how much they don't know. After all, they say, "I've had pets all my life." One of our jobs as rescuers—in fact, our most important job—is to do what we can to shine some light on the dark sea of ignorance and misinformation.

PREVENTING AND CORRECTING PET PROBLEMS

Although detailed discussion of behavior issues in different kinds of animals and possible solutions are beyond the scope of this book, it's worth noting that many problems are related to the following factors:

- Lack of exercise: This applies particularly to dogs, but can also be a factor for cats and other animals whose energy runneth over. Most pet owners overestimate how much exercise their pets get, and underestimate how much exercise their pets need.

According to Sue Gilsdorf, Ratuie had "nearly every behavior problem in the cat book" when his previous owner took him to the shelter. Sue adopted him and trained him with a clicker, and he obviously loves her enough to jump through hoops. PHOTO COURTESY OF SUE GILSDORF.

- Boredom: This is a factor particularly in animals that spend a lot of time alone and confined without sufficient mental stimulation. Exercise helps, as does training. Most pet dogs get only rudimentary training, and most other pets get essentially none.

- Physical problems: Many pets have health problems that affect their behavior, including parasites, disease, injuries, allergies, hormonal imbalances, dental problems, ear infections, and so on. A thorough exam by a vet who is informed about the animal's behavior problems and who will look for physical causes may make all the difference.

- Nutritional problems: Poor nutrition, as well as food allergies and sensitivities, can cause behavioral problems, including incessant itching, hyperactivity, lethargy, and others. Food-related problems are quite common, and do not occur just in animals fed bargain basement foods—some of the "premium" brands contain grains, dyes, preservatives, and other ingredients that have been tied to behavior issues.

Heredity, pre- and post-natal care, socialization, and early environment and handling can be factors, too. Although you cannot change them, knowing as much as possible about an animal's background may help you help the owner find ways to stop or lessen the unwanted behaviors. Conversations about these aspects of choosing a pet also offer opportunities to educate people about responsible breeding, buying, socializing, and training. The more people understand about those things, the more likely they are to make good choices that reduce the need for rescue.

Sometimes it takes a bit of detective work to figure out why an animal is (mis)behaving in a particular way, so take a close, open-minded look at the animal's environment, either in person or by asking lots of questions. Cat avoiding the litter box? Strong-smelling cleaners and air "fresheners" might be driving him away. Dog driving everyone nuts with his itching? Those nightly popcorn snacks could be the culprit. Bunny suddenly jumpy as well as hoppy? Could be an infection in his ears or head.

If you can point to possibilities that unhappy owners haven't thought of, you may provide an easy fix and keep the animal in his current home. If not, and assuming that the owner would like to keep the pet but not the problem, recommend a consultation with a veterinarian, behaviorist, or knowledgeable breeder or owner—or all of the above. Sometimes several factors work together to cause a behavior pattern, and several approaches combined may be needed to change it.

SUPPORTING YOUR ADOPTERS

Your relationship with your adopters should continue for the remainder of the adopted animal's life. That doesn't mean you have to talk once a week (although for the first several weeks that's an excellent idea), but all adopters should feel that "their" rescue group is a resource they can use whenever they have questions or concerns about their pets. Here are some methods that established rescue groups have found useful for maintaining relationships with adopters:

- Standard post-adoption follow-up procedures (*see* Chapter 10).
- Newsletter that goes to all adopters, donors, and volunteers—include stories about adopters and their pets.
- Periodic get-togethers, with or without pets—perhaps an annual picnic.

You can support your rescued animals and their new people, too, by providing them with information and updates about resources in their communities (vets, obedience trainers, clubs, businesses, and others who support rescue or offer useful services).

Finally, you can assure your adopters that should they die or become unable to care for their adopted pets, you will gladly take them in and find them new homes if necessary. Indeed, rescuers (like breeders) should be willing to take back any animal they have placed if the need arises. After all, by rescuing them, we become responsible for the animals that touch our lives.

CHAPTER

8

Health Screening and Care

Animals coming into a rescue organization must be screened medically for their own welfare, and for the safety of caretakers, adopters, and other foster animals and pets. Isolation and careful screening are not signs of paranoia but part of caring responsibly for foster animals and our own pets, whose health and safety should be our highest animal-related priority.

Some rescued animals arrive with up-to-date veterinary records, but most do not, and this great medical unknown always represents risk. Even when an animal appears to be healthy or has a known history, you don't know what he's been exposed to that could be incubating. That's why every newly rescued animal should be isolated from other animals, and examined as soon as possible by a veterinarian.

A good working relationship with one or more veterinarians is fundamental to rescue work. This doesn't mean that the vet will give free services or even reduce her fees, although freebies and discounts are great. It's more important, though, that the vets with whom you work are willing to answer questions and give sound, practical advice, and that they are accessible immediately for emergencies and within a reasonable time frame for other services.

SETTING UP STANDARD PROCEDURES

Your volunteers should follow a standard intake protocol when accepting new animals (*see* "Establishing Policies and Procedures" in Chapter 1), and should record what was done, when it was done, and by whom—to ensure that all steps are taken, and to establish records for all the animals you handle (visit www.rescuematters.com for forms that you can download free of charge). Having individual written records can be invaluable for tracking a particular animal's condition, and, if an animal becomes ill after adoption, will show that you took appropriate precautions and treated the animal as your vet advised.

The specific procedures your group follows will depend on the species or breed you handle, where you are, where each animal was before you took him in, and other factors. Consult one or more veterinarians and talk to other experienced rescuers so that you can make informed decisions, using the suggestions that follow as a starting point.

Rabbits, Rodents, and Exotic Animals

Most of the information in this chapter refers to dogs and cats. If you rescue rabbits, rodents, birds, reptiles, any type of exotic animal, or large animals, routine screening and care will be a bit different, as will signs of trouble. Not all vets are skilled in treating all creatures, so the first thing to do is find a vet who is experienced with your type of animals. You can also obtain information and lists of recommended reading from established rescue groups as well as organizations devoted to breeding and showing.

Isolate New Animals

Ideally, animals should be examined by a veterinarian *before* entering foster care. Realistically that isn't always possible, so your foster caretakers should be educated about how to protect their own pets and human families. In general, the following procedures will help keep everyone safe and healthy.

Prevent direct contact between new fosters and other animals. Use crates or kennel runs that can be disinfected between animals, and provide a place for new rescues to potty where other animals don't have access. Isolation is especially important if the new guy is a stray, arrives very dirty, or was taken from a dirty environment. Exercise extra caution if he has any of the "Signs of Trouble" enumerated in the next section.

- Ideally, volunteers and members of their families will wash their clothing in hot water and bleach, disinfect their shoes, and take hot, soapy showers after all encounters with incoming animals or their quarters. Most people won't be so fastidious, but they should at least avoid contact with other pets until they can change clothes and shoes and wash their hands thoroughly.

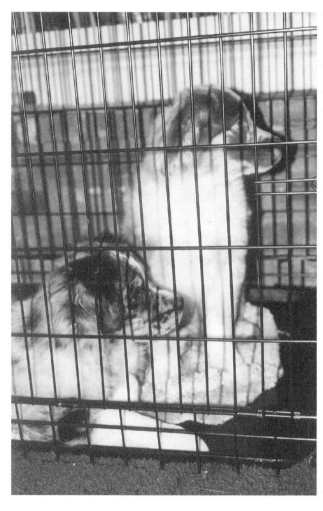

These eight-week-old Australian Shepherd puppies were rescued by the author and her friend Vicki Webb on behalf of a local Aussie rescue program. Their parents were owned by a man whose grasp of canine knowledge was infirm, to say the least—he told us (among other nonsense) that Aussies are the long-haired version of the Australian Cattle Dog. When he couldn't sell all the pups, he released these two to rescue. After a short period of isolation from other pets, they were both adopted. PHOTO BY SHEILA BONEHAM.

Screen for Signs of Trouble

Animals entering rescue often have parasites and other health issues that you may not know about at first, so a veterinary examination should be scheduled, and the animal should be screened as appropriate for parasites and other problems. Even if you take animals to the vet promptly, your volunteers will do some initial screening. The details will depend on the animals you rescue, but the following points apply to most. If you use a checklist, give your vet a copy when you take the animal for an examination.

Skin and Coat

Check for signs of parasites; note any lumps, bumps, sores, wounds, tender areas, bare spots, or other skin problems; remove debris, tangles, and matts from the fur; note the condition of the coat (dry, brittle, sparse); groom and bathe as necessary.

Weight and Condition

Record the animal's weight and note whether he is underweight or overweight. Teach your volunteers to recognize when an animal is in proper weight—many pets are obese because people don't know how to assess weight properly. Too much or too little weight can be a sign of disease or other serious health problems, but usually it is directly related to food intake. Neglected animals are often too thin from lack of food, disease, and/or parasites, or, ironically, too fat from unmonitored food intake and lack of sufficient exercise. Note any other signs of poor physical condition.

Ears

Healthy ears are free of discharge, foreign matter, swelling, inflammation, sores, and irritated skin. Head shaking, scratching or pawing at the ears or head, carrying the head at an odd tilt, foul odor, and obvious tenderness or sensitivity may indicate ear problems. Don't guess or use over-the-counter or home remedies—the wrong treatment can be worse than none at all. If the ears are dirty but show no signs of infection, clean them gently with a commercial ear cleaner or with cotton pads soaked with hydrogen peroxide. Never probe parts of the ear that you can't see—you could injure delicate tissues.

Eyes

Healthy eyes are clear and the area around them is clean. If you see redness, irritation, excess tearing, discharge, or swelling, see your vet. In the meantime, clean accumulated gunk gently with cotton pads moistened with water. Use a clean pad for each eye. (Don't use cleansing balls with fibers that could get into the eyes.)

Mouth

Many animals enter rescue with gum disease and, sometimes, damaged or, in the case of rabbits and rodents, overgrown teeth. If you can do so safely, check each animal's mouth; if the animal resists, seems to be in pain, or seems likely to bite, wait for the vet. If possible, have tooth problems taken care of and include the cost in your adoption fee. Otherwise, advise adopters about any existing problems. If an animal will need extensive dental treatment after adoption, you may want to reduce the adoption fee.

Feet

Many animals enter rescue in desperate need of pedicures. Overgrown, torn, split, or ingrown nails damage feet, interfere with mobility, and cause pain; they need to be attended to as soon as possible. Depending on the animal, the condition of his feet, and his past experience, you may be able to trim the nails yourself, or it may be a "three-volunteer job." (Some critters make it worth the money to have an experienced veterinarian or groomer do their nails!) Some animals have other foot problems, including damaged pads and other injuries that may need veterinary attention.

Anal Glands

Dogs, cats, and many other animals have anal glands located at the sides of the anus. These glands produce scented matter that is normally released when the animal defecates. If a gland becomes *impacted*, or blocked, it fails to drain, causing discomfort or pain. Signs of anal gland problems include licking or biting at the anal area, scooting the rear end across the floor, or a foul odor. Your vet can teach you to relieve mild impaction by *expressing*, or emptying, the glands. If impacted anal glands become infected, indicated by blood or pus in the secretions, the animal needs antibiotics. If the infection becomes an *abscess*, which appears as a red or dark purple swelling at the site of the gland, it needs immediate veterinary care.

HEALTH ISSUES

Comprehensive health information is clearly beyond the scope of this book, so I've chosen to present very basic information on a few serious problems that rescuers are likely to see at some time. As always, work closely with one or more veterinarians whom you trust, and encourage all volunteers who handle animals to learn as much as possible about how to prevent and manage health issues. If you rescue purebred animals, check with the parent club, as many clubs support health research and provide excellent, up-to-date information of use to rescuers as well as owners and breeders.

Some signs of ill health require immediate action for the good of the affected animal and for other animals around him. Diarrhea, bloody stools, and vomiting are among the most serious not only because they may indicate life-threatening illness but also because of their potential to spread infectious disease and parasites (not to mention their ability to turn off volunteers). Let's start there.

Diarrhea

Diarrhea is caused by irritation of the small or large intestine. Severe diarrhea, or diarrhea accompanied by vomiting, can cause life-threatening dehydration, especially in young or small animals, making immediate veterinary care essential. Some common causes of diarrhea include the following:

* stress
* bacteria

- viruses
- parasites
- change of diet
- ingestion of garbage, grass, or other indigestible substance (*see also* "Intestinal Obstruction")
- nutritional deficiency
- inflammatory bowel disease
- toxins
- antibiotics
- pancreatitis

It's not unusual for rescued animals to experience short-term stress-induced diarrhea. As long as the animal shows no other signs of illness, one or two loose stools are probably not serious. Still, it's best to isolate him from other animals, and get him to a veterinarian as soon as possible for diagnosis and treatment. If the diarrhea is severe or lasts longer than a day, if you see blood or foreign matter in it, or if the animal is young, small, or has other symptoms, treat the situation as an emergency.

Often diarrhea can be stopped by withholding food for 24 hours to rest the intestine, and then feeding a bland diet for a day or two. The regular diet should then be slowly reintroduced by mixing the bland diet with normal food, slowly increasing the proportion of the latter and decreasing the former. Do *not* give over-the-counter anti-diarrheal medications without asking your vet.

Bloody Stools

Blood in stools can indicate serious problems. The appearance of the blood will depend on where in the digestive tract it originates. Black stools often indicate bleeding in the stomach or small intestine. Reddish or rusty stools usually indicate bleeding lower in the digestive tract. Red spots or streaks on the surface of stools may indicate bleeding low in the large intestine or rectum.

Although fecal blood may be visible to the naked eye, often it cannot be detected or verified without chemical analysis—another reason that fecal examinations should be part of every rescued animal's initial screening.

Constipation

Constipation often results from swallowing indigestible material such as bones, plant matter, or hair, although some animals simply refuse to defecate in strange places. Whatever the cause, failure to have a bowel movement in 24 hours can lead to serious complications.

Aside from the obvious lack of poop, other signs of constipation include loss of appetite and sometimes other signs of illness. In rabbits, sparse or tiny stools strung together by hair can indicate a life-threatening hairball.

If an animal fails to have a bowel movement for more than a day, call your vet. *Do not* administer laxatives unless advised to do so by your vet—if the intestine is blocked, a laxative could be lethal (*see* "Intestinal Obstruction" later in this chapter).

Vomiting

Upchucking may or may not be a sign of trouble. Regurgitation of recently ingested food often occurs after an animal bolts food, drinks too much water too quickly, or becomes stressed. Cats often barf up hairballs. Although it is often not a cause for alarm, vomiting can indicate a serious problem. The following situations require veterinary attention as soon as possible:

- Vomiting Blood: If an animal vomits bright red blood, or partially digested blood that looks like coffee grounds, get to a vet immediately.
- Vomiting Feces: Vomit that smells of feces may indicate an obstruction of the intestinal tract or an abdominal injury, either of which require immediate veterinary care. Keep in mind, though, that *coprophagia* (feces eating) is not uncommon, and if the animal has ingested feces, he may throw it back up. If in doubt, see a veterinarian.
- Projectile Vomiting: Vomit that shoots violently from the mouth may indicate a blockage in the upper gastrointestinal tract, or any of a number of other serious problems. See a vet immediately.
- Vomiting Foreign Objects: Vomiting of foreign objects—rocks, worms, rawhide, pieces of bone, pieces of plastic or rubber toys, or other non-edibles—requires an emergency trip to the vet to make sure there's no more where that came from.
- Sporadic Vomiting: Sporadic vomiting that does not appear to be linked to meals, especially when coupled with diarrhea or listlessness, requires veterinary attention.

Seizures

A *seizure* occurs when nerves in the brain "fire" suddenly and without normal controls, causing muscles to contract repeatedly. Although they are terrifying to watch, and animals can injure themselves during an episode, seizures are rarely fatal in and of themselves. However, in extreme cases, an animal may exhibit *status epilepticus* (seizure after seizure), and without time to rest and recover, may suffer hyperthermia (overheating), hypoglycemia (low blood sugar), exhaustion, permanent brain damage, and death.

It's important that your volunteers know how to manage seizures, and that as a group you are aware of possible causes and solutions. Unfortunately, seizure behavior is often diagnosed as "epilepsy" without consideration of other potential causes, especially in breeds with a high incidence of inherited seizure behavior. In fact, seizures can result from a range of causes, including:

- poisons
- drugs

- head injuries
- fever
- heat stroke
- congenital defects
- tumors
- diabetes mellitus
- hypoglycemia (low blood sugar)
- kidney or liver disease
- infectious disease
- other factors

The first step in stopping seizure activity is to identify the cause if possible. Work with your vet, and gather as much information as possible about the animal's background and his environment prior to each seizure. If the cause can be identified and removed, the seizures will probably stop. If not, and if your group can afford the cost or find a sponsor for the animal, work with a veterinary neurologist who can make a detailed diagnosis and develop a treatment plan.

If the cause of the seizures cannot be identified, the animal is said to have *idiopathic epilepsy* (meaning that the cause is unknown), which is generally considered to be hereditary. Often the seizures cannot be stopped completely, but their frequency and severity can be controlled so that the animal can live a reasonably normal life. Any potential adopter for a pet who has seizures should be advised about the need for ongoing veterinary care for the animal, including administration and close monitoring of anti-seizure medications and periodic blood chemistry and liver function analyses.

Volunteers who handle animals should learn how to manage a seizure. In general, the following guidelines apply:

- Remain calm.
- Write down the starting and ending times.
- Keep away from the animal's mouth—he could bite without even knowing it. (Don't worry—he won't swallow his tongue.)
- Move sharp or hard objects out of his way, or cushion them with pillows or blankets to protect the animal.
- Remove or turn off nearby stimuli, including bright or flashing lights and loud music or noise.
- If children are present, they need to be quiet. (Adults too.)
- Reassure the animal by touching him gently and speaking calmly.

Although they seem to go on forever, most seizures last only a few minutes. As soon as the seizure ends, call your vet. If the seizure lasts more than fifteen minutes, or if one seizure follows another, wrap the animal gently in a sheet or blanket to keep him from thrashing around, and take him to your vet or an emergency clinic.

Bloat

All canine rescue volunteers (and dog owners in general) should know that *gastric distension* caused by a stomach overly full of food or gas can quickly become life threatening if the pressure makes the stomach twist, causing *gastric dilatation-volvulus* (GDV) or *gastric torsion*, or, in popular parlance, *bloat*. When the stomach twists, it seals off the esophagus and prevents the dog from belching or vomiting to relieve the increasing pressure. Blood flow into and out of the heart decreases and arterial blood flow to the stomach is reduced, causing the stomach lining to die. Toxins build up, damaging the liver, pancreas, spleen, and bowel. In some cases, the pressure ruptures the stomach. The spleen often twists with the stomach, and may have to be removed. Without immediate treatment, the dog suffers considerable pain, goes into shock, and dies.

Any dog can bloat, but dogs with deep chests have increased risk. Signs of bloat or impending bloat include any or all of the following:

- distended abdomen
- lack of appetite
- retching without bringing anything up
- drooling
- lethargy
- restlessness
- pacing and refusal to lie down
- depression
- weakness
- rapid heart rate

Instruct your volunteers to act *immediately* if they think a dog may be bloating. They should call ahead to alert the vet, then get there as quickly as possible. Surgery and follow-up care can run to thousands of dollars, so if you rescue a breed that has a significant incidence of bloat, you need a written policy on treatment (*see* Chapter 1). Be clear about how much you can spend, how the immediate cost will be covered so that a volunteer isn't on the spot, and who will make the decision to euthanize the animal if necessary.

Allocation of Rescue Resources

Diseased and injured animals raise practical and ethical questions for rescue groups. We've all heard stories of remarkable animals who have survived incredible injury or illness, and we all want our less fortunate charges to have a chance at a healthy life. But rescue groups must balance the financial and human resources that will be exhausted in rehabilitating one extremely needy animal against the number of healthier animals that could be fostered and saved with those same resources. It is never easy to make such a call. Sometimes it needn't be made at all—for example, if you can find donors to cover an animal's expenses and volunteers to provide the care the animal needs. Unfortunately, though, sometimes the bottom line really is the bottom line. We must also ask how much an animal should be allowed to suffer, and what constitutes a quality life. In short, we must be sure when we take extraordinary measures that they are in the animal's best interest rather than our own.

Many dogs die of bloat even with surgical intervention, so prevention is by far the best medicine. Two or three smaller meals a day rather than one big one, and restricted exercise for at least two hours after meals, reduce the risk of bloat.

Intestinal Obstruction

Animals sometimes eat things that have no business being in a digestive system. If they get stuck, the animal can suffer an *intestinal obstruction* or *blockage*, which is a true emergency.

Signs of blockage include vomiting or retching, diarrhea, listlessness, distended or tender abdomen, loss of appetite, and/or constipation.

If you know or suspect that an animal has a blockage, or has swallowed something that is unlikely to make the journey through the digestive system on its own, call your vet immediately. She may prefer to watch and wait at first, but surgery may be necessary. Again, your policies and procedures should cover such situations.

Urinary Problems

Urinary incontinence refers to *involuntary* urination that occurs when the animal cannot control the passage of urine from the bladder. This should not be confused with *frequent urination*, in which the animal has to go frequently but retains control, or *submissive urination* (*see* Chapter 9). Some pet owners can't deal with an animal's loss of control, and leave it to rescuers to do so.

Incontinence can have any of a number of causes, including:

- Disease or deformity of the urinary bladder or the urethra.
- Brain or spinal cord injury, disease, or abnormality.
- Partial blockage of the urethra.
- Lack of certain hormones after altering (easily correctable with medication and not a legitimate argument against spaying or neutering).
- Malformation of the vagina (*vulvovaginal stenosis*).

- Age-related weakening of the sphincter muscles that control release of urine from the bladder.
- Age-related dementia.

Treatment and prognosis for incontinence depend on the cause, and the animal himself, so veterinary care is essential. At the opposite extreme, if an animal stops urinating, or appears to strain or to be in pain when attempting to do so, he needs emergency veterinary care.

PREVENTING DISEASE

Risk of exposure to specific diseases varies by species, location, and other factors, so work with your veterinarian to decide what inoculations and other prophylactics are necessary for the animals you rescue. Be sure that your vet understands that you want the animals protected from common diseases, but that cost is also a factor. Adopters can have optional vaccinations given later if they so choose.

Rabies

Of the few diseases we can catch from our pets, the most frightening is *rabies*, a viral disease that can attack any mammal. Once symptoms appear, rabies is always fatal, so prevention is essential. The rabies virus is transmitted in the saliva of infected animals, is endemic in populations of wild animals in North America and elsewhere, and is passed easily to domestic animals.

Rabies affects the central nervous system and takes two forms. *Furious rabies* is what most of us picture—an aggressive animal foaming at the mouth. But the disease can also take the form of *dumb rabies*, which paralyzes the lower jaw, then the limbs, and finally the vital organs.

Common sense and the law dictate that rabies vaccinations are essential for many kinds of pets, particularly dogs and cats. How frequently they should be given is a topic of much debate, though, and a rabies vaccine challenge test is currently underway to determine how long vaccinations are effective.

Other Vaccinations

Other recommended vaccinations depend on the species and risk of exposure. If an animal arrives with a record of up-to-date vaccinations given by a licensed veterinarian, there is no reason to re-vaccinate. In fact, research shows that excessive vaccination may compromise an animal's long-term physical and mental health. As a result, the American Veterinary Medical Association (AVMA), the American Association of Feline Practitioners (AAFP), most veterinary colleges, and many veterinarians and owners have changed their approaches to pet vaccinations. Discuss the needs of the animals you rescue with your vet, and provide information and resources for your volunteers and your adopters so that they can make informed decisions about vaccinating their pets.

PARASITES

Even well-cared-for pets may have parasites, and rescued animals that have been neglected or housed outdoors will almost certainly be infected. That's a problem for the rescued animals and for the people and animals they meet.

Encourage your volunteers to speak to their veterinarians about parasite control for their individual circumstances. In general, the following procedures will go a long way toward prevention and control.

- Have fecal specimens for all incoming animals checked by a veterinarian (*see* "Initial Screening" in this chapter).
- Have fecal specimens for all long-term foster animals and volunteers' pets checked periodically (ask your vet about recommended intervals).
- Keep yards clean and lawns cut short to control fleas.
- Pick up feces at least once a day and dispose of them properly.
- Treat all new arrivals for intestinal parasites as recommended by your vet, even if their fecals are negative (which means that no eggs were seen in the specimen; immature parasites could be present but not yet producing eggs).
- Isolate newly rescued animals until they get the all clear (*see* "Isolation" in this chapter).
- Clean and sanitize crates, carriers, kennel runs, bedding, floors, and concrete and gravel surfaces as recommended by your vet.

Now let's take a look at common parasites and what you can do about them.

External Parasites

Fleas
Fleas spread disease and other parasites, and aren't fussy about who they bite. In animals with allergies they cause severe itching and secondary infections. I'm sure they have a purpose in the grand scheme of things, but to my mind the only good flea is a dead flea.

Check all newly rescued animals for fleas *before* they enter a foster home or interact with other animals. If you find one flea, you can be sure she's not alone. To prevent a population explosion, you need to kill the adults and their eggs and larvae on pets, in the home and yard, and possibly in vehicles. Ask your vet to recommend safe, effective products. Don't use over-the-counter or homemade remedies and don't combine different products without veterinary guidance.

Unless there is a medical reason not to do so, bathe animals that have signs of fleas. You don't need to use insecticidal shampoos—in fact, they can be dangerous for puppies, kittens, and animals with health problems. Using regular shampoo labeled for the type of animal you are bathing, make a ring of lather around the neck right behind the ears to prevent fleas from moving to the head. Lather the body, legs, and tail, and leave the lather on for ten minutes to drown the fleas. Comb through fur on the head and remove any fleas you find with the flea comb or your fingers. Drop the fleas into a container of water (a drop of detergent will break the surface tension and prevent the fleas from staying on top and leaping to freedom). When the bath is finished, flush the captured fleas.

Ticks

Ticks are arthropods (relatives of spiders) that eat blood and spread disease. Ticks are widespread in wooded and brushy areas, and can be carried into your yard by wild and domestic animals. From there it's an easy trip into your home.

If you find a tick on an animal or person, remove it *carefully*. If it has not attached itself to the skin, pick it off with a tissue. If it is attached, dab it with iodine, alcohol, or a strong saline solution on a cotton ball to loosen its grip. Then grasp its body as close to the head as possible with forceps, tweezers, a tissue, or a special tick remover (available from some pet-supply stores). Pull gently *straight out*. Don't squeeze—you could force disease-bearing liquids from the tick into the victim. Flush the tick down the toilet, or seal it in a plastic bag and dispose of it. Clean the area with alcohol, Betadine, or iodine, and apply an antiseptic. Wash your hands and any tool you used with soap and hot water. Watch the bite for a few days, and call your vet or physician if you see signs of infection or rash.

Mange

Mange is the common term for several skin conditions caused by microscopic arthropods called *mites* that eat skin debris, hair follicles, and tissue, typically causing their victims to lose hair and develop flaky, itchy, crusty skin. Animals with mange often scratch themselves raw, opening the way for secondary invasions of bacteria, viruses, fungi, and other parasites. Some types of mange mites will attack people.

To treat mange effectively, the species of mite must be identified, so again, don't waste time and money on homemade or over-the-counter treatments. Take any animal with bare or irritated skin to your vet.

Ringworm

Despite its name, *ringworm* is a highly contagious fungal infection. The first sign of ringworm is usually a sore-looking bald circle.

Ringworm, like other fungal infections, is hard to treat. Home remedies and over-the-counter treatments are rarely effective, and just give the infection more time to take hold and to spread to other animals (or people). Your vet can prescribe effective treatment, and tell you how to limit spread of the infection.

Intestinal Parasites

Intestinal parasites are extremely common. Their effects on the health of the host animal vary from minimal to life threatening. Although they may cause no obvious symptoms, intestinal parasites can cause diarrhea, sometimes with blood in the stool, weight loss, dry skin and coat, vomiting, and the appearance of generally poor health.

Many parasites cannot be detected without a microscopic examination of a fecal specimen, but animals with heavy infestations often expel worms in feces or vomit. If that happens, grit your teeth and put some in a bag to show your vet so that she can prescribe the appropriate medication.

For treatment to be effective, the parasite must be accurately identified. Some parasites are hard to eliminate, so additional fecal exams and treatments may be necessary. Work with your vet to eliminate intestinal parasites, and advise adopters about follow-up exams.

Some parasites can be transmitted to people, so proper hygiene is critical, especially careful hand-washing after handling the animals or cleaning up after them. Feces should be picked up and disposed of frequently, and living and elimination areas should be sanitized regularly.

The MDR1 Mutation, Seizures, and Drug Sensitivity in Dogs

Heartworm preventatives are generally safe and can protect dogs and cats from devastating heartworm infestations. However, certain drugs can cause seizures, other neurological complications, and death in dogs that have a genetic mutation known as the *MDR1 Mutation*. As of this writing, the MDR1 Mutation is known to affect the following breeds (and mixes that include these breeds): Collies, Australian Shepherds (Aussies), Shetland Sheepdogs (Shelties), Old English Sheepdogs, German Shepherd Dogs, Long-haired Whippets, Silken Windhounds, and a variety of mixed-breed dogs. As more dogs are tested, it is likely that more breeds will be added to the list. Drugs known to cause problems in some dogs with the MDR1 mutation are:

- *Ivermectin,* used to prevent and treat heartworm, mange, and other parasitic infection.
- *Selamectin, milbemycin,* and *moxidectin,* used in several heartworm preventatives.
  Author's Note: Manufacturers and research from the Veterinary Clinical Pharmacology Lab at Washington State University College of Veterinary Medicine state that the dosages present in heartworm preventatives are

safe. Anecdotal evidence from owners of some affected breeds, though, suggests that prolonged usage of these drugs can result in adverse reactions.

- *Loperamide,* the active ingredient in Imodium™ antidiarrheal medication, should never be given to pets.

The following drugs are usually safe if given in reduced dosages with veterinary supervision.

- *Acepromazine,* a tranquilizer and pre-anesthetic agent.
- *Butorphanol,* an analgesic (pain killer) and pre-anesthetic agent.
- *Vincristine, Vinblastine, Doxorubicin,* which are chemotherapy agents.

Researchers also recommend that the following drugs be given to dogs with the MDR1 mutation only with caution and close monitoring: Domperidone, Etoposide, Mitoxantrone, Ondansetron, Paclitaxel, and Rifampicin.

Adopters should be informed about the potential problem, and about the possibility of having their dogs tested for the mutation. To do so, they need only swab the dog's inner cheek with a special brush and mail it in for analysis. For more information, contact Washington State University College of Veterinary Medicine, Veterinary Clinical Pharmacology Laboratory, PO Box 609, Pullman, WA 99163-0609; Phone/FAX: 509-335-3745; Web site: http://www.vetmed.wsu.edu.

Heartworm Disease

Heartworms are parasitic worms that infest the heart. Heartworm larvae are carried by mosquitoes from infected animals to others. The larvae move through the blood vessels to the heart, where they mature. As their numbers increase and the individual worms grow, they fill the space available, causing congestive heart failure. Because of the small size of the feline heart, a single heartworm can kill a cat.

Heartworm disease has been diagnosed in all fifty states and beyond, so all dogs and cats taken into rescue should be tested for heartworms, even if the relinquishing owner says the animal has been on preventive medication. Testing for other animals may or may not be recommended, so if you rescue animals other than dogs or cats, ask your vet.

Effective preventive medications are available, but rescued animals older than six months should not be given a preventative without prior testing because if worms are present in the heart, the preventative can be lethal. Recommendations for beginning heartworm prevention in puppies and kittens varies with the different drugs, but are generally four to six weeks of age, so check with your vet and read the product information sheets, many of which are available on line from the manufacturers. Even if babies begin taking preventive medication very young, when they are seven or eight months old they should be tested for heartworms acquired earlier. The *microfilaria* (heartworm larvae) take about six months to develop into reproducing adults, so a test done less than six months after the microfilaria enter the body will appear negative. Some dogs are sensitive to ingredients in some heartworm treatments and preventatives (*see* "The MDR1 Mutation, Seizures, and Drug Sensitivity in Dogs"), so choose your poison carefully.

Most vets recommend retesting for heartworms annually since no medication is one hundred percent effective. Two types of tests detect heartworms. A *filter* or *Knott's* test is a microscopic examination of blood under a microscope to see if microfilariae are present. With an *antigen* test, the blood is checked for antigens (substances that stimulate the creation of antibodies) produced by adult heartworms. Antigen tests are preferred for diagnosis because a significant number of heartworm-infected dogs and cats have no microfilaria. However, antigen tests are also more expensive than filter tests, which is a factor for many rescuers. If you cannot afford to use antigen tests, ask your vet's advice about using preventive medications and advise adopters to have their pets tested with their initial post-adoption exams.

Treatment for heartworm disease is expensive, labor intensive, and hard on the animal. Drugs are given to kill the adult worms, and animals must be kept quiet during treatment. One of the policy decisions your group should make in advance is whether, and under what circumstances, you will treat animals that test positive for heartworm disease (*see* Chapter 1).

ALTERING

All animals placed through rescue should be altered (with rare exceptions due to medical reasons). Your policy statement and adoption contract should be explicit and unequivocal about this requirement. Responsible breeding is essential to the future of healthy, high-quality pets, but rescue organizations must never be a source of breeding animals.

Ideally, all rescued animals should be altered *before* they go to their new homes. Realistically that isn't always possible, due to financial and other constraints. Some animals arrive with medical problems that preclude immediate surgery, and for some baby animals, early altering is not the best option (*see* "Early Altering: Yes or No?").

Early Altering: Yes or No?

Many shelters, rescue organizations, and breeders favor early (juvenile) altering at as young as seven weeks. Although it seems like a perfect way to ensure that animals

One day in May 2007 my dogs told me there was "something" under our deck. That something turned out to be a cat with a very young kitten, one of four born under a neighbor's deck; only one made it to the more secure den behind our house. Gypsy, as I call her, soon learned to trust us to feed her, talk to her, and eventually touch her, and she brought her kitten out three weeks later. He went to a wonderful indoor home when he was 14 weeks old (see photo in Chapter 10), and we had Gypsy spayed and vaccinated. Although Gypsy comes to visit often, she wants no part of life indoors. Sometimes we can only do so much. PHOTO BY SHEILA BONEHAM.

adopted young are unable to reproduce, there are drawbacks to early altering. Not all veterinarians are skilled in anesthetizing or operating on baby animals. In addition, lack of sex hormones in adolescence prolongs the growth period. For small animals this may not be a problem, but I can tell you from personal experience that altering medium to large dogs at two months can seriously affect physical development, causing them not only to grow considerably taller, but to have abnormally elongated, narrow heads and narrow bodies, and to lack normal muscular development. Your policy on early altering should hinge not only on the importance of preventing unwanted litters, but also on the welfare of the individual animal and the people who will love him. An enforceable altering contract may be a better option.

If you find it necessary to place an intact (unspayed or unneutered) animal in an adoptive home, have an attorney review your adoption contract to be sure the altering requirement is enforceable. As with other provisions of the contract, consequences should be specified for failing to alter an adopted animal, and those consequences must be reasonable under the law or they will be meaningless. Your contract should require the adopter to send you verification of the surgery signed by a veterinarian.

Assign a volunteer to check that all adopters send their verifications in a timely manner, and to call or send reminders to those who do not. Some people simply forget to send the paperwork. Give them two to three weeks after the reminder to comply. If you still don't receive the paperwork, send a polite but firm letter reiterating the terms of the adoption, and the reason for the altering requirement. That usually does the trick. If not, have your attorney write a letter, and be prepared to enforce your contract in court if necessary. Keep copies of everything you send, and a log of non-written communications.

Although a frightening array of health issues can arrive on your doorstep, most rescued animals have only minor problems that are easily addressed. Your job is to establish policies and procedures to manage the difficult cases, work with one or more veterinarians, and educate your volunteers about health management for rescued animals and their own families, human and otherwise. Finally, include health care information in your adoption packets to help adopters keep their new friends as healthy as possible for as long as possible.

CHAPTER

9

Temperament and Behavior

Many animals find themselves in rescue, in shelters, or dumped on country roads because their owners perceived them as being badly behaved. Sadly, many "bad" behaviors have more to do with the owner's lack of knowledge or failure to provide for the animal's needs than with the animal's true temperament. Many young dogs, for instance, lose their homes because of behaviors that result from lack of sufficient exercise and/or training. Many cats lose their homes over elimination issues that could be solved by changing or moving the litter box. And so on. In some such cases, owners can be educated and the "family" preserved (*see* Chapter 7). If not, the animal's behavior can often be radically altered by foster caretakers and adopters by addressing his or her physical, mental, and emotional needs.

Screening of rescued animals for behavioral quirks is vital for several reasons. The adopter deserves an accurate picture of the temperament and behavioral challenges, if any, of his pet. As importantly, the reputation and future of your rescue organization depends in part on the animals you place into the community. Finally, the reputation of the species or breed you love rests on the behaviors of the individuals who represent it to the public.

This chapter focuses on general temperament and behavior issues that are critical in rescue work. I encourage all rescuers to learn as much as possible about positive training approaches to help them work with rescued animals, and with owners who might be helped to keep their pets. Temperament and behavior, although not the same thing, are intertwined, and temperament sets the stage, so we'll begin there.

TEMPERAMENT

Temperament is the general attitude an individual animal shows towards other animals, people, and the world in general. Temperament is inherited, but it can be modified or enhanced by the environment. A shy kitten may never be a social butterfly, but can gain confidence with careful handling and socialization. A dominant puppy can become a mannerly, outgoing dog or a domineering, even aggressive animal, depending on his owner's ability to train and manage the dog's behavior.

Your volunteers should learn as much as possible about the ideal temperament of the species or breed with which they work. This "normal" temperament is as much a part of the animals' characteristics as are coat length, size, and colors. It's essential to understand, though, that any population will include animals with a range of individual temperaments. Many of these variations, while not ideal, can be considered normal for the particular breed or species. A few animals, though, will have temperaments that are atypical for the breed (or, sometimes, species).

Temperament affects an animal's suitability for placement as a pet, and deviations from the norm should be considered on a case by case basis. For instance, although Abyssinians are typically very active, somewhat vocal cats, a quiet couch-potato Aby would certainly be placeable. On the other hand, a rescued Golden Retriever who growls and snaps at children must be placed with extreme caution, if at all, because even if the dog goes to a home with no children, he will encounter them in public places. And because Goldens are expected to be "friendly, reliable, and trustworthy" and not hostile to dogs or people in normal circumstances, adults who might restrain kids from approaching some dogs would tend to be less concerned about a Golden Retriever.

With careful, knowledgeable handling, an animal whose temperament is fundamentally sound can overcome many deficits in his pre-rescue life. Animals with truly problematic temperaments are another thing. Even with proper handling and training since birth, poor temperament may cause unacceptable behaviors. When an animal has had less-than-optimum training and care, as is the case with many rescued animals, then poor basic temperament, often coupled with lack of socialization, can lead to insurmountable behavioral issues, the most serious of which is aggression.

AGGRESSION

The most serious behavioral problem encountered by animal rescuers is aggression—that is, attacks involving teeth and, in some cases, claws or other potentially injurious body parts. You won't always know about the problem until the animal is in foster care, because some relinquishing owners prefer to let rescuers experience the joy of discovery themselves. Other owners will tell you that the animal has bitten several people, but they just don't want to put him down. In either case, the owner is unwilling or unable to deal with the problem but is willing to pass it on to someone else. Finally, some people may know in their hearts that the animal should be euthanized, and your role will not be to handle the animal but to help the owner reach that heart-rending decision.

Aggression takes many forms and springs from many sources. For organized rescue programs, the bottom line is that putting an animal who has a known history of aggression, or who behaves aggressively while in rescue, into foster care or an adoptive home carries legal and moral liability. Therefore every rescue program needs to establish policies on taking in and fostering aggressive animals and rehoming them.

Some groups accept such animals, evaluate the background information, observe the animal, and then decide whether to euthanize or try to rehabilitate and rehome. Other groups will not accept any animal that has bitten a person, and some will take the animal and have him euthanized. If you know when you take in an animal that you may have to euthanize him, be honest about that possibility. You may be sorely tempted to lie in some cases, but doing so will only damage the reputations of all rescue programs and the people who work so hard on their behalf. By the time they come to rescue, many owners of aggressive animals know that their pets are dangerous, but cannot face the decision and the act. You don't need to say that you're going straight to the vet, but neither should you pretend that you will place a dangerous animal in a new home.

Part of rescue's burden of public education is making people understand that aggression, especially when aimed at people, is not normal or acceptable in pets any more than it is in our own species. As a rescuer, you must remember that every animal you foster or rehome represents your species or breed, your rescue program, and pet rescue in general. Remember, too, that aggressive pets do not live happy lives. They often lose home after home and may endure physical and emotional punishments. Finally, as rescuers we have a moral responsibility not only to the animals in our care, but to the people in our communities and their pets. Putting them at risk of injury from an animal we know to be dangerous is inexcusable.

Owners (and inexperienced foster caretakers) frequently misinterpret animal behavior. A cat that becomes over-stimulated by petting and responds in typical feline fashion by grabbing someone's arm may be labeled "aggressive." A puppy that hasn't been taught not to grab human fingers with his teeth when playing may be labeled "vicious." A bunny that bites because he has a raging ear infection may be labeled "mean." An animal who was never properly socialized and who has become a fear biter, snapping when strangers try to pet him, is "nasty." And so on.

Many pet owners also inadvertently encourage or reinforce aggressive behaviors like resource guarding in their pets, and such animals often respond well to retraining.

Medical problems, such as chronic pain, hormone imbalances, or neurological problems, may also be linked to aggressive behavior. Ultimately, every case must be evaluated on its own merits, ideally with the help of a veterinarian and/or qualified behaviorist.

HEALTH RELATED BEHAVIORAL PROBLEMS

Some behavioral issues spring from medical problems, many of which can be cured or controlled with proper diagnosis and treatment. Whenever a rescued animal displays undesirable behaviors that are not obviously the result of the environment or lack of training, you need to look for physical causes. Realize, too, that one problem often generates another, so dig deep when you look for causes and cures.

Suppose, for example, that Rover has a chronic allergic skin condition. He's allergic to corn, but no one has ever told his owner that the popular food he feeds his pet is making him ill. Rover's scratching drives his owner nuts, and the ear infection brought on by the allergy smells yucky. The owner relegates Rover to the back yard. Lonely and bored, Rover becomes a recreational barker, irritating his owner and everyone else within five blocks. Desperate for company, Rover goes wild whenever anyone enters the yard—his owner has bruises to prove it. Rover escapes the yard and lives up to his name, costing his owner several bail-out fees at the local shelter. Dog and owner are both frustrated.

Or maybe Benjamin Bunny has begun biting and going nuts when anyone tries to pet him. He used to be such a sweet bunny, but now no one can get near him. The owner hasn't thought to take him to the vet, who would have found the ear infection that has spread to his face. It hurts when people touch him.

Enter rescue.

Orthopedic problems, chronic or acute pain, hormonal imbalances, food allergies, diseases of various internal organs, impacted anal glands, parasites, dental problems, ear infections—almost anything that makes an animal feel bad may cause him to behave in ways that people find objectionable. Train your foster caretakers to be alert and observant, and always tell your vet about behavioral issues in your rescued animals and ask about possible underlying physical causes.

OTHER COMMON BEHAVIORAL PROBLEMS

Most pet owners would be shocked and insulted if you accused them of neglecting their pets, but the fact is that neglect of one sort or another is a leading cause of behavioral problems in pets. Neglect doesn't necessarily mean shoving an animal into the backyard or failing to provide proper care (although those actions certainly qualify). In most cases of neglect-induced behavior problems, the underlying causes are less

Woody was adopted from a county shelter as a young adult stray, but was surrendered a year later for possible euthanasia due to behavior problems, including aggression. Despite his issues, Denise Whitfield decided to give Woody another chance. Denise, who had trained many dogs to top competition levels, soon realized that Woody was a very intelligent, high-energy dog who lacked confidence. Denise felt he needed a job: competition obedience. Woody thrived on reward-based obedience training; his aggression issues were managed with socialization techniques developed by world-renowned dog trainer Sylvia Bishop, and Woody became confident and relaxed around other dogs. He excelled in competition, earning the coveted title of Obedience Trail Champion (OTCh) and many national honors in both AKC and St. Hubert's CDSP competition obedience programs. On May 4, 2008, I had the honor of watching this lovely dog earn his AKC Tracking Dog title at the age of 12 years, making him the first rescued Golden Retriever to earn both the OTCh and the TD. Woody's registered name is now OTCH OTCH-H Res-Q-Me Your Favorite Deputy UDX, UDX-H, TD. Photo courtesy of David Whitfield.

Training benefits most animals, and many of them embrace the power of working for rewards with great enthusiasm. Here Olive Oink demonstrates how she has trained owner Andrea Cole to hand over the corn puffs when she sits pretty. When Andrea was training her pup, Olive watched, then came and sat. Did someone say treats? Since then Olive has learned to pirouette on cue, and she is currently learning to negotiate an agility obstacle course, along with the two dogs. (See more of Olive in Chapter 3.) PHOTO BY SHEILA BONEHAM.

shocking to the average person's sensibilities but just as devastating for the animal whose behavior becomes intolerable for his owners. Neglect in this sense includes the failure of owners to socialize, train, and exercise their pets' bodies and minds.

Team Up with Experts

In Chapters 1 and 8, I discussed the importance of teaming up with at least one veterinarian. Karen Dunn, a volunteer with Almost Home Dog Rescue of Ohio, Inc., a 501(3)c Collie rescue program, recommends that rescue groups also partner with qualified trainers and/or behaviorists. She writes, "Working with a trainer has saved us time and heartache, and has helped us get dogs adopted. We've had several dogs evaluated, and have had two stay with the trainer at her home, which is also her training facility. She does charge us, but half of her normal rate. It's really been an enormous help to us."

Some people who really want to keep their pets can be re-educated and rehabili-tated along with them (*see* Chapter 7). When this is not the case, you'll be comforted to know that once they enter environments that address their physical, emotional, men-tal, and social needs, most "problem" pets become wonderful companions. The need to ensure that those needs are met is, of course, another reason that it's important to match foster animals to the right caretakers, and adopted animals to the right adopters.

This is not a book on training and behavior. That said, let's survey a few common behavior problems seen in rescued animals.

Inappropriate Elimination

Soiling in the house is one of the most common behavioral issues leading people to give up their pets, especially dogs and cats. Most house-training problems are caused by incomplete training, environment, conditioning, or physical problems.

Many dogs are sent packing by owners who never really taught them where they should and should not go. Many cats lose their homes for going outside a litterbox that was difficult for them to use, dirty by feline standards, or otherwise uninviting (*see* also Chapter 7). Fortunately, most pets can learn proper elimination etiquette even as adults, especially if the underlying problem is lack of effective training or uninviting "facilities."

Dogs, cats, rabbits, and most other animals naturally prefer to urinate and defe-cate away from where they sleep and eat, but animals that have lived in filth often be-come indifferent to it. Fortunately, most can be reconditioned. How quickly an individual learns to like being clean and living in clean surroundings will depend on how long the animal lived in filth and on his individual personality.

To set an animal on a cleaner path, create an environment in which it's difficult for the animal to be wrong, and help her form good habits. Most eventually come around, so be patient. Finally, be especially careful when placing such an animal in foster care or an adoptive home—caretakers and owners must understand that the animal (through no fault of his own) needs remedial house training. As always, if retraining seems to take longer than it should, have your veterinarian examine the animal.

A number of health problems can cause inappropriate elimination. Spayed bitches sometimes dribble urine, and relatively inexpensive, low-dose estrogen therapy usu-ally stops the problem. Kidney and bladder infections can cause urinary problems in dogs, cats, and other animals, and a variety of diseases, infections, parasites, and other factors can make urinary and bowel control difficult or impossible (*see* Chapter 8). If house training takes longer than you think it should, or if an animal breaks house training after being reliable, speak to your vet.

As we saw with health-related behavior issues, lack of proper house training is often related to other problems. A cat who won't use the litterbox because of stresses in his environment may also engage in other undesirable behaviors, such as destruc-tive scratching or aggressive behaviors. A dog that soils the house may find himself out of the house or confined to a room away from the family. Bored and lonely, he may bark, dig, chew, and rip things up. Problems beget more problems. By the same token, addressing the root of the problem behavior often has a ripple effect—fix one problem and others often miraculously disappear.

Submissive Urination in Dogs

Submissive urination is not a house-training problem and should not be treated as such, but many owners of submissive dogs don't understand the distinction. In canine language, subordinate individuals urinate as part of the ritualized behavior they use to signal submission to more dominant animals. A dog that is naturally shy or submissive often uses this same behavior to signal submission to people. The dog thinks he's being extremely polite; his people think he's making a mess.

The problem escalates if people react by yelling or punishing the dog, who simply pees more to see if that will make folks happier. Submissive urination is not uncommon in rescued dogs, and such individuals should be fostered or adopted by people who are sensitive to the dog's responses and who don't mind cleaning up a little peepee while the dog gains confidence.

Some submissive dogs never completely stop urinating when greeting people and other dogs, but most can learn to do it less often and less copiously if they are handled with patience and understanding. Caretakers and visitors should tone down any actions that the dog may perceive as dominant behavior likely to trigger the urination response as a sign of submission. Avoid direct eye contact, especially when approaching the dog. Rather than bending over the dog, squat or sit near him. If he shows any inclination to bite when frightened, keep your face out of range and never chase or corner the dog (*see* "Aggression" in this chapter). Scratch the dog under the chin and on the chest, which he will perceive as less dominant behavior than head petting. When returning home after an absence, greet the dog calmly and wait a little while before petting him. Use positive, motivational training techniques, and make any necessary corrections quietly, calmly, and gently. Guests should be asked to follow the same guidelines when interacting with the dog. If they can't manage to do so, put the dog in his crate in a quiet place before they arrive.

Lack of Socialization

Young animals must learn to interact effectively with others, and every species has a critical developmental period for becoming properly *socialized*, or acquainted with the world around them. Unfortunately, many people unwittingly fail to socialize their pets properly during the critical time slot, and many animals become excessively shy or aggressive out of fear or lack of social skills, or both. Lack of socialization is especially a problem in dogs because they are likely to encounter people and other dogs on walks and at home, but cats, rabbits, and other pets that lack social skills can also develop problem behaviors that land them in rescue.

Although we can't completely compensate for missing critical socialization periods, with patience and time most animals that have fundamentally sound temperaments can learn the social skills they need to interact with others comfortably and effectively. Careful introductions to people and well-socialized pets of their own kind can work wonders. Positive obedience training is of obvious benefit for rescued dogs, and helps build confidence and social skills. While perhaps not so obvious, positive training also benefits cats, rabbits, and other pets, as it builds their confidence in the trainer and exercises their bodies and minds. So-called "clicker training" (operant conditioning in psychological terms) is very effective with all kinds of animals, and knowing a few cute tricks certainly can't hurt an animal's appeal to potential adopters. Besides, learning to train an animal is great fun for foster families and adopters alike, and the respect and trust that the process builds is one of the best tools you have for helping undersocialized animals learn to function in society.

Separation Anxiety

Separation anxiety refers to a condition in which an animal becomes agitated when left alone or, in some cases, when separated from a particular person. In his effort to deal with the stress, the animal may develop undesirable behaviors ranging from mildly annoying to destructive and dangerous, including vocalizations, pacing, neurotic licking or self-mutilation, excessive salivation, vomiting, inappropriate elimination, and destructive chewing, clawing, and ripping up of whatever he can find. Unfortunately, many people perceive these behaviors not as responses to stress, but as the animal's effort to "get back at" their owners. Some animals come into rescue because their owners can't live with the anxiety-induced behaviors but don't know how to correct them. Others develop some degree of separation anxiety as a result of losing their homes, especially if they spend time in a high-stress environment before entering foster care. Either way, separation anxiety is a fairly common issue in rescued animals.

Effective treatment for separation anxiety requires time and patience. The first step is to ensure that the animal is safe when he must be left alone, and that he can't damage any important property in his foster home. Crates work for most animals, although some don't like the close confinement and do better in a larger kennel run or secure room. If a particular animal seems likely to injure himself when alone, your veterinarian can prescribe an anti-anxiety medication, but drugs are not the best long-term solution.

Behavior modification should always accompany drug therapy, and is often effective by itself. What you need to do to help any particular animal will depend on the animal's background and history of separation anxiety and other factors. If necessary, ask your vet for a referral to a behaviorist who is knowledgeable about the type of animal you rescue and about treating anxiety disorders.

Destructive Behavior

Destructive behavior is a common problem in rescued animals, and is often brought on by one or more of several factors, including boredom, lack of exercise, lack of training, too much freedom, or separation anxiety (*see* previous section and Chapter 7).

When you rescue an animal with a history of destructive behavior, which the previous owner may or may not disclose, your first priority must be to protect the animal himself, and the property he may damage. Be sure that his foster caretaker knows about the problem, and will be able to follow through with a program to prevent destructive activity and redirect the animal's energy and behavior.

Don't conceal an animal's behavior problems from potential adopters—your job is to match the animal with a new owner who is committed to continuing the process of prevention, training, and redirection.

Performance Sports for Rescued Dogs

If you rescue dogs, consider providing information to adopters and potential adopters about opportunities to train for and compete in canine sports, which promote two of the essential components of successful dog ownership: training and exercise. Behavior problems can be often be prevented or overcome by a combination of exercise, bonding, and giving a dog a job. Many rescued dogs compete successfully and earn titles and honors in performance events (obedience, agility, tracking, and certain breed- or group-specific sports) through a number of sponsoring organizations. To participate, each dog must be registered with the organization itself or another acceptable registry—owners should check the requirements of each group of interest. The United Kennel Club (UKC) (www.ukcdogs.com) and the Australian Shepherd Club of America (ASCA)(www.asca.org) welcome all dogs, purebred and mixed-breed, into their performance competition programs. The American Kennel Club (www.akc.org) offers a limited form of registration to enable altered dogs that appear to be purebred to participate in AKC performance sports.

CHAPTER

10

Rehoming Rescued Pets

Careful screening of potential adopters is essential if you are to find responsible, loving homes for the animals in your charge. The key to careful screening is a systematic, multifaceted process involving checks and balances. The specific concerns will vary, naturally, according to the species, breed, and individual, but the same general principles apply to all animals. An effective screening program aims to ensure that each animal will receive companionship, affection, proper nutrition, exercise, regular veterinary care, a safe living environment, and as much "education" as necessary to be a well-mannered, confident member of society.

ATTRACTING ADOPTERS

Although the word is definitely out about canine rescue programs, many people are still unaware that there are rescue programs for almost all breeds of dogs and for cats, rabbits, rodents, birds, reptiles, exotic pets—not to mention the bigger guys who can't live in the house. Whatever your rescue animal(s) of choice, if you want to match them with the right adopters, you have to make your presence known.

Advertising is one option (*see also* Chapter 4). Different kinds of ads bring difference responses, so experiment to find the best approach for your area and animals. General ads, such as, "Beautiful adult cats, occasional kittens, seek loving homes with qualified adopters. Maine Coon Rescue & Placement, web address, e-mail, telephone number," will make your presence known, help raise awareness, and result in some adoptions. Many rescue groups also get results from ads describing two or three specific animals. Consider this one, for instance:

Lab Love Lines: Special guys looking for special homes. Elvis, a blonde hunka burnin love with big brown eyes; Joe, black male, sports fanatic (tennis, soccer, football); Shadow, strong silent type, loves to snuggle, take walks, and play with kids & cats. All dogs neutered, current on health care, looking for qualified permanent homes. Lab Rescue, [e-mail, web site, phone number].

State that the animals mentioned and others are available to *qualified* adopters, and provide copies of your adoption policy along with other information to potential adopters (*see* Chapter 1).

Your web site is one of your best tools for attracting adopters because you can post not only information, policies, and application forms, but also photos of available animals, success stories, and perhaps other special rescued animals.

There are also Internet sites devoted to getting the word out about adoptable rescued animals, and you can link notices you post to your own web site. One caution—the last time I posted a notice on an adoption clearinghouse site, my mailbox filled with Nigerian-based scams and not one legitimate inquiry. So I recommend you start slowly, with one or two postings, and then decide whether the service is worthwhile for your group.

SCREENING ADOPTERS

The combined experience of hundreds of rescuers has shown that the biggest challenge is not attracting would-be adopters but separating the good candidates from those who would be better off with a different kind of animal, or no animal at all. Here are some common screening methods, and some suggestions to make the screening process more effective.

E-mail and Telephone Screening

In most cases, the initial contact between adopters and your rescue program will be by e-mail or telephone, and it is in that early communication that the screening process begins for both parties.

E-mail is an extremely convenient means of communication in these busy times, but because they lack the many clues to meaning that we pick up when we hear someone

In May 2007, Bob's mother Gypsy (see Chapter 8) took up residence under our deck with her newborn kitten. We spent lots of time with the little family, fed them and played with them, and had them examined and vaccinated. Gypsy had no interest in being an indoor pet, but she let us handle and socialize Bob ("Born Out Back"). To his mama's obvious disgust, Bob spent a lot of time inside our house and fraternized with the dogs before moving to his new indoor home with two feline friends, where he's known as Bunky. PHOTO BY SHEILA BONEHAM.

on the phone or (better) in person, e-mails messages can also miscommunicate. At some point, an adoption counselor needs to speak to each potential adopter. (*See* Chapter 1 for more on effective e-mail communication.)

For some people, the telephone will still be the first and possibly only means of communicating with your group prior to a home visit or "meet-the-animal" visit. For others, it will be an intermediate step between applying to adopt and a face-to-face meeting. To make telephone screening more efficient and consistent, each volunteer should use a standard set of questions to ask and points to mention. The questions may simply reiterate your written adoption application (*see* "Formal Application"), but re-posing them will allow your volunteer to ask for clarification if the applicant's meaning is hazy. It will also give the would-be adopter a chance to ask as well as answer questions that come up in the course of the conversation.

If a caller will obviously not qualify to adopt one of your animals, tell him so politely but clearly, and give him a reason based on your written policies (*see* Chapter 1). Your heart may long to holler that you wouldn't hand a plastic animal over to him, but limiting yourself to a policy-based rejection ("we only adopt to people with fenced yards") is a better choice in the long run.

If the caller does seem appropriate but has not yet made formal application, send him your information and application, or refer him to your on-line forms.

Formal Application

Formal application to adopt an animal should be made in writing. Most adoption applications are from one to four pages long, with the specific questions and level of detail determined by the animals you rescue and the policies and philosophy of your group.

Your application form will probably evolve over time, but you can get started by borrowing (with permission) another group's form (or visit my web site at www.rescuematters.com for a generic form that you can modify for your own purposes). In general, a good adoption application:

- Asks why the person wants the pet and who else will be part of the pet's life.
- Explores the person's history of owning, breeding, and rehoming pets, including those he has currently.
- Determines whether the person is able and willing to provide proper care for the pet and to abide by your group's adoption policies.
- Confirms that the person understands the specific characteristics and requirements of a pet of this type.

Be sure that the questions on your application are clear and, when screening applications, be sure you understand the answers. Consider this rather shocking misunderstanding over an applicant's answer to one of our screening questions. The question was, "Why do you want a Labrador Retriever?" The would-be adopter was a biology professor, and his answer to the question was "Research." Gasp! But the volunteer who read the application had also conducted the original telephone screening, and had thought the man sounded decent, so she call to "verify" his written answers. She asked what he meant when he said "research," and he said, "Well, my wife and I read a number of books on choosing a breed, and we've read some things about Labs, and we think this will be an excellent dog for us." Whew! That was a relief, and a reminder that it's easy to miscommunicate and misunderstand.

That works both ways, of course, so always be sure that potential adopters understand your adoption policies as you mean them. Does your "fenced yard" policy include underground electronic fences? Does "indoor pet" mean the cat or rabbit can never go outdoors? And so on.

References

Ask for references. If the applicant has owned an animal before, one of the references should be a professional person who knows something about how the animal was cared for—perhaps his veterinarian, groomer, or obedience instructor. All of the references should have personal knowledge of the applicant's relationship to animals. (If the applicant has not had a pet before, or if it's been a long time, ask for references who have animals with which the applicant has interacted.)

Check some, if not all, references. Legitimate adopters have no problem referring you to people who know them. Unfortunately, neither do many illegitimate applicants. I heard about one guy who apparently assumed that no one would check—he gave a veterinarian and an obedience instructor as references, but neither one had ever heard of the person.

Sometimes information about an applicant pops up unexpectedly and can be useful, perhaps alerting you to something that would disqualify the applicant from adopting from your group. Double (or triple) check negative information, though, especially from on-line sources, where attacking people for all sorts of reasons has become a sport for some. This goes as well for so-called "do not adopt" lists that circulate on the Internet. Sometimes the information is accurate and well founded, but sometimes it isn't, and accusations once posted take on a life of their own. I've been targeted myself, and it's a nasty business often fueled more by jealousy and other emotions than by fact. So if you get negative feedback about an adoption applicant, check it out, but cautiously. Ask the applicant directly, without revealing your source, for his version of the story—it may be very different from what you've heard—and have at least one volunteer visit his home. Then it will be up to you to weigh all the information you have and decide.

Home Visits

Ideally, one of your volunteers will visit the applicant's home before the person is approved to adopt. I often take a well-behaved dog as "co-interviewer" because people's reactions to an animal in their own homes can speak volumes. Request that all members of the household be present, and observe each person's behavior with the animal carefully. Pay special attention to how much control the parents have over their children, and how it is exerted. People who can't control their kids, or who are overly harsh with them, are likely to act the same way with a pet.

To ensure consistency regardless of who visits each home, develop a checklist for evaluating the suitability of the environment for an adopted pet. You can also use the list to suggest changes that might improve certain aspects of approved homes—for instance, "We recommend that you move the bone china flower collection from the coffee table to a more secure location."

Home visits may seem a waste of time, especially when the applicant appears to fit all of the criteria, but visits sometimes reveal the unimagined. We once had applicants who sounded perfect—in fact, one of our volunteers worked with the husband, had met his wife, and thought that they would be fine adopters. They already had a five-year-old, medium-size male mixed breed, and they wanted a second dog. They had two children, aged nine and fourteen, a fenced yard, and an active lifestyle. Sounded perfect for a Labrador Retriever—until we visited. We took along a dog that we thought they might like, planning to check out the house and yard, then take the dogs to a nearby park to introduce them. When we arrived, their dog was in a crate, and the father told the kids not to let him out. The nine-year-old boy immediately released the dog, which ran to our car (parked on the street) and started a ruckus. The situation went downhill from there. The children were completely out of control. The swimming pool took up most of the backyard, and we were afraid that a Lab would get under the cover and drown. The adults were offended when the dogs sniffed each other's behinds, and paid no attention when we tried to explain the behavior. If we had used only their written application, telephone interview, and references, we would have approved the adoption. Because of what we saw during the visit, they did not get a dog from our group.

Home evaluation is an area where inter-rescue cooperation can pay off, especially if volunteers for different groups are willing to educate one another. Say Persian Cat Rescue needs a home check done miles from its nearest volunteer. With a checklist and some cat education, maybe a Corgi Rescue volunteer can make the visit. Not only does such networking simplify things for your group, but it provides opportunities for volunteers to learn more about animals and rescue work beyond their usual sphere, and, in rescue as elsewhere, knowledge is power.

Approving and Declining Applicants

Approving and disapproving applicants is not an entirely straightforward process. Some people or families are clearly suitable or not suitable to adopt the pets in your care, but others are more difficult to assess. Perhaps they don't meet some specific criterion, but otherwise seem like excellent candidates. Or maybe they seem to meet all the requirements, but some little tickle in your gut makes you reluctant to say yes. (I've learned to pay attention to these gut feelings, by the way.) Perhaps the volunteer who conducted the initial interview or home evaluation is uncertain about an applicant, or two volunteers who performed different parts of the screening can't agree. Now the decision becomes more difficult.

How you handle these situations will depend on the specific situation, and possibly on how many animals you handle and how difficult they are to place. You may choose simply to decline applications that don't earn a resounding A-OK. But, as with your questionnaire, things aren't always what they seem to be, so you may want to arrange for one or possibly two other volunteers from your own group to visit the home and follow up to clarify points from the questionnaire and/or previous interview. Sometimes it pays to have a volunteer drive or walk by the applicant's house at an unscheduled time. They won't be able to get in, but might see something important.

Telling people that are they are approved is an easy, pleasant duty. Giving bad news isn't so nice, but it is necessary. It is unfair, and unprofessional, to leave someone hanging just because you don't like to say "no." Sometimes you can soften the blow by suggesting another breed or type of pet that might suit the applicant better. Give reasons if you think they're useful and not insulting—"rescued pets need considerable attention, which we don't think will be possible with your busy work and travel schedule" or "we are concerned for the safety of a dwarf rabbit with your three terriers." Otherwise, simply say that in your opinion the pets you handle are not suitable for the person's situation. Leave it at that, even if you're sorely tempted to say more. Your energies are better spent in positive ways.

MATCHMAKING: THE RIGHT PERSON FOR THE RIGHT PET

Some pets and people seem made for each other, and matches are easy. Other times, it takes a while to find the right pet for an adopter, or the right adopter for the pet. Easy or hard, placement choices should be based on careful assessment of each animal's behavior, temperament, and needs, and each adopter's personality, experience, living situation, and stated tolerance for specific traits of animals. One person's dream pet is another's nightmare, and it's your job to help make dreams come true with careful placements.

The more your foster caretakers learn about animal behavior, and the more they can interact with and observe the animals in their care, the more accurately your group will be able to assess each animal's needs. Accurate assessments will lead to more successful adoptions. Not only can you choose adopters who are more likely to accept an individual animal's quirks, but you can also counsel your adopters about each animal's temperament and potential issues and how better to manage them. Such attention takes some time and effort, but can make the difference between adoptions that work and those that don't. It's definitely a win-win-win situation for your group, your adopters, and—above all—your animals.

ADOPTION CONTRACTS

Some people will tell you that an adoption contract is "no better than the people who sign it." In some ways, that's true, especially if the contract is not written in a way that makes it legally binding. Even if it is properly written, a lawsuit to enforce a contract may be too expensive for a shoestring rescue group to pursue.

On the other hand, a well-written contract does several things to protect your rescue group, the adopter, and the adopted animal. It spells out the terms of the adoption so that all parties (except the animals!) understand them. It guards against the

Hunting beagles who have gotten too old to hunt are often simply abandoned in the woods or at the side of a road. The lucky ones are picked up by animal control. The really lucky ones are picked up when a rescue group has an opening. Dudley was one of these—but just barely. On the day he was scheduled for euthanasia, Beagle Rescue of Southern Maryland decided they had room for one more dog. As an older dog, he didn't arouse much interest, and he was with Beagle Rescue for over a year before he was adopted by Linda Coleman, who had prior good experiences with senior dogs and was specifically looking for an older dog who would be a good Pets on Wheels visitor. Dudley—aka "Boogie Woogie Beagle Boy"—now visits a local nursing home, helps with special programs on pet care in schools and clubs, and, with housemate Riley (see Chapter 2), participates in two local libraries' Read to Rover programs. PHOTO BY SHEILA BONEHAM.

memory lapses that come to most of us with time. And it specifies what will happen if either party fails to fulfill the terms of the contract. In general, a good adoption contract includes the following points:

- The parties to the contract.
- A description of the animal (species, breed, color, sex, age, microchip or tattoo information if pertinent, and other identifying characteristics).
- The adoption donation or fee.
- The terms of the adoption.
- Penalties for violations of the terms.

- A venue statement specifying where any legal action to enforce the contract will be taken.
- A statement specifying who will be responsible for paying the cost of enforcing the contract if that becomes necessary.
- A statement indicating that the contract is the complete and sole agreement between the parties concerning this adoption.

To ensure that your adoption contract is legally binding, consult an attorney—preferably one who is familiar with both contract law and laws pertaining to pets.

GOING HOME

Sending rescued animals to their new homes is always a stressful, albeit exciting, experience for everyone involved. There are some things you can do to ease the process.

Encourage people to pick their new pets up when they will be able to spend some time together—Friday evenings and Saturday mornings work well for many people, giving them the weekend to get acquainted. The settling in process will vary depending on the type of animal, his age and background, and the adopter's situation, so advise your adopters as appropriate.

A week or so before the big day, send the adopter information about his new pet. Sending it in advance increases the likelihood that the adopter will read it. If you wait until adoption day, the animal will take center stage. Would you want to stop to read when you could be getting to know your new friend? What you send will depend on available resources, the species or breed you handle, and other factors. Here are some ideas:

- A sheet describing "what we know about" the adopted animal.
- Animal's veterinary record.
- Guide to using a crate or cage.
- Suggestions to help the animal get settled.
- Nutritional information (give a small starter supply of food on adoption day).
- Registration information if the animal is tattooed or microchipped.
- Copy of the rescue group's newsletter.
- Catalogs for discount pet-supply companies.
- Printed information or a book about the species or breed.
- A list of recommended books, magazines, and web sites.
- Information on what to look for in a veterinarian.
- Information on parasite control.
- For dogs, a guide to what to look for in an obedience instructor, and a list of recommended instructors or behaviorists.
- A list of suggested safe toys, and warnings about toys that might be dangerous.

Post-adoption Veterinary Examination

All adopted animals should be examined by a veterinarian within two or three days after they go to their new homes. A short but reasonable time frame makes it unlikely that the pet will acquire a health problem between adoption day and the exam. Remind adopters to give copies of existing vet records to their own veterinarians—there's no point re-vaccinating or performing tests that have just been done. Be sure to specify in your adoption contract that the examination will be at the adopter's expense and that it will not be reimbursed by your group.

The post-adoption check-up accomplishes several things. Hopefully, it assures the adopter that the animal is healthy, and it provides the vet with baseline information. It's always possible for an exam to detect a problem that wasn't found earlier. Rescue groups should be willing to take back any animal with a health problem for a full refund or for an alternate animal when one becomes available. If the adopter chooses to keep the animal, your group will have to decide whether to pay part or all of the cost of treating a pre-existing but previously undetected condition.

Some rescued animals have obvious, sometimes serious, health problems. Your program may choose to treat the animal or, in severe cases, to have him euthanized (*see* Chapters 1 and 8). But sometimes people come along who will adopt, love, and care for ill or injured animals. If you place an animal who needs veterinary and nursing care, describe the condition in the adoption agreement (attach a veterinary diagnosis and preliminary treatment plan) and specify that the adopter will pay for treatment and care. In such cases, it may be appropriate to reduce or even waive the adoption fee.

Saying Farewell

The departure of a rescued animal from his foster home is often a bittersweet occasion. Foster caretakers and their families develop very close attachments to the animals in their charge, and the animals to them. And yet, something astonishing happens when adopters pick up their new pets. Perhaps they read our minds and hearts, but somehow, the animals seem to know. I've seen many a clingy foster animal leap into an adopter's car and leave without a backward glance. It's that leap of faith and hope that we all work to achieve through rescue work.

The best advice that I can give is to prepare first-time foster caretakers for that big goodbye. Recommend hankies. Remind them that they are not losing a friend, but making new ones. Point out that now there is room to foster another and save another. Tell them to have a good cry, then clean everything up so that they'll be ready for the next rescued animal that needs love and safe harbor.

FOLLOW-UP PROCEDURES

Adoptions should be followed up at regular intervals to be sure that everything is running smoothly and that any contractual obligations (such as post-adoption neutering or obedience training) are being fulfilled. Aside from reassuring you, such follow-ups reassure the adopters. Sometimes small problems develop, and people are too shy to call and ask for help. By the time they do, the small problem may have become a big one. Follow-ups also demonstrate that the rescue group takes its job seriously and that you are available to support your adopters.

The day after the animal goes home, someone should call to make sure that the first night went well and to ask if any help or advice is needed. I would recommend another call after a week, another after a month, another after six months, and then annual calls on or close to the adoption anniversary. A portable file box can be used to set up a "tickler file" of post-adoption check sheets. A simple way to establish such a file is to get twelve file folders and label one for each month. Place the current month at the front. When the month ends, move the file to the back, and work through the check sheets in the next month's file. This creates a system that reminds volunteers of adoption anniversaries and other important dates in the life of a rescued animal. When a particular animal's check sheet is brought up-to-date, place it in the appropriate file for the next scheduled follow-up. The anniversary of the adoption is a nice occasion to remember. Send a card to arrive that day, then have a volunteer call to congratulate the adopter and animal and to do the annual follow up.

CHAPTER

11

Optimism

The most appropriate long-term goal that an animal rescue organization can set is to reduce the need for rescue. Although it seems unlikely that any of us will do this in the near future, we can try. In Chapter 7 we looked at how we can try to help one pet owner at a time, and in Chapter 5 we explored some ways to publicize your group, rescue in general, and responsible pet care. As we wrap up this book, I'd like to toss out a few more ideas.

Set an example. Give priority to the welfare of your own pets, the ones to whom you have made a long-term commitment. They should be well-groomed and in proper weight, and fit as appropriate for their ages. They should be properly socialized and trained so they can understand how you want them to behave, and they should get enough exercise to channel their energy in safe, positive directions.

If you choose to purchase your own dogs, cats, rabbits, birds, or other pets, deal only with responsible breeders. If you adopt from shelters or rescue programs, choose as much with your head as with your heart. Remember, and be able to articulate to other people, that life with an animal should enable both to live optimally. Many breeds, mixes, species, or types of animals may fill our eyes and make our hearts beat faster, but that doesn't mean we each can provide the environment that every sort of pet needs.

Be an omnivorous consumer of information about animals, not just the breed or species you own and rescue, but others as well. Learn as much as possible about animal health, nutrition, behavior, and training, and be able to refer people to sources of accurate information when necessary.

When people admire your pets, mention that the glossy coat comes from good food and regular grooming. When they seem astonished at how well behaved your dog is, talk about the hours you spend on positive, motivational training, and how without daily exercise the dog is a dervish. Explain that, yes, this is a lovely breed of dog or cat, or a cute creature of another sort—unless you work long hours and can't manage boundless energy, or you don't like pet hair in everything, or whatever else might make your favorite pet inappropriate for someone else. Helping one person understand that pets are not interchangeable may not seem like much, but if it keeps one animal out of the wrong home and out of rescue, it's really quite a lot.

If you have volunteers with the time, talent, and inclination, arrange to visit schools or youth groups to talk to children—the pet owners of the future—about everything from safety around animals to lifelong responsible care. Take a well-behaved animal if possible. Not only will you light up the eyes of the children (and their teachers), but they will carry home some of the information. If there is a college in your community, distribute literature there and inquire about opportunities to speak to students (and faculty and staff) about rescue- and pet-related topics. The effects can reach farther than you may think.

Sometimes rescue work seems hopeless. We work and work, and still the animals keep coming. Some people seem to be willfully ignorant about pets, buying "designer breeds" and dealing with pet stores, puppy mills, and others who profit from the suffering of animals and the people who love them. Yet I think there is reason for hope.

More people than ever before are making well-considered choices and getting their pets from responsible sources. More people than ever are taking their dogs through basic obedience courses and becoming involved in sports like agility and obedience that foster training and channel energy. More and more people keep their cats indoors, where they live longer, safer, healthier lives. More people than ever before have begun to recognize that all animals can be trained with positive methods, which creates a small but profound shift in thinking about these animals and how they should live. For many pet owners, spaying and neutering have become as basic as feeding a pet or picking up poop.

Great changes in societies start small, and while the rescue road is long and often dark and bumpy, we have covered considerable ground. And beside us, always, to make the journey worthwhile, are the companions of our hearts.

Appendix

1

Sample Documents

A number of sample documents, as well as other resources, are available for free download on my web site at www.rescuematters.com. Samples of two that are frequently used are on the following pages.

ADOPTION APPLICATION

Note: This is a generic sample form — you may want to add or omit questions specific to the species or breed that you rescue. A template that you can modify is available at www.rescuematters.com.

Our Rescue Group   E-mail us at e-mail@ouraddress.com
Ourtown, U.S.A.   1-800-call-now
On the web at OurRescueGroup.com

Your tax-deductible adoption donation will help defray the cost of rescuing and rehoming the animals. Please note: We place animals only within 25 miles of Ourtown.

Adopter's Information

Your name:
Your complete address (not a post office box):
Home phone:
Work phone:
Cell phone:
Preferred number: ___Home ___Cell ___Work   Best time to call:
E-mail address (please indicate if you do not have e-mail):

Occupation:
Employer:
How long have you been at your present job?
If less than 1 year, how long at previous job?
Who else lives in your household? Please provide names and ages of all
    household members under 18 years of age.

Why do you want this type of pet?
Do you understand that Fuzzyfaces shed and some are noisy?
Do all members of your household want to adopt a pet of this type?
If not, please be specific about who disagrees, and why.
Is anyone in your household allergic to this type of animal?
If so, how do you plan to manage the allergy?

Is your home a ___House ___Apartment ___Condominium ___Mobile home
    ___Other
Do you ___Own ___Rent ___Other (please explain)

How long have you lived at this address?
If less than 2 years, what was your previous address and how long did you live
    there?

If you rent, do you have your landlord's permission to keep a Fuzzyface?

Landlord's name:
Landlord's phone:
Landlord's address:

Does your community have any laws or covenants restricting the number or
    type of pets you may own? If so, will you be in compliance if you adopt a
    pet from us?

Do you have children? If so, what experience have they had with pets?

Who will be the primary caretaker for this pet?

Do you have regular visitors with whom your pet will need to interact?
    Please be specific.

What other pets currently live in your household? For each, please specify
    species, breed (if known), size, age, and who owns each, and which animals
    are spayed/neutered and which are not.

On a separate sheet, please list each pet you have owned in the past 10 years:
    please give name, sex, breed, if spayed/neutered, where you acquired each
    one, the years you owned each, and what happened to each of them.

Have you ever given up a pet?_____Yes_____No

If so, why? Please be specific.

What did you do with the pet? Have you or anyone in your household ever been convicted of cruelty or neglect?_____Yes_____No

Have you ever received a pet-related citation or been fined for violating a pet-related law?_____Yes____No
(If you answered yes to either question, please attach a complete explanation.)

How large is your yard?   Is it completely fenced?
Type of fence: Height of fence:
How do you secure your gates?

If you do not have a fence, how do you plan to keep your new dog safe and in compliance with confinement laws?

Do you have a swimming pool or hot tub?
Is it fenced separately from the rest of your yard?
Does it have a secure cover that a pet cannot get under?

How many hours per day will your pet spend:

____in the house? ___in the garage? ___in the yard?

____in an outdoor kennel or cage?

____in a specific room or area of your house? (Which room or area?)

Will your pet be restricted from any particular parts of your home or yard?

How many hours a day will your pet spend without human companionship?

Will your pet have the company of other pets? Please be specific.

Where will your pet be when no one is home?

Who will care for your pet when you are away from home overnight?

Does anyone other than family/household residents come into your home on a regular basis (for instance, a cleaning service)?

If so, how will you ensure your pet's safety when outsiders need to come and go?

Have you ever lost a pet, either temporarily or permanently? (Do not include death from illness or old age.)

If so, what happened?

If you own a pet now, or have owned a pet within the past 10 years, please provide at least one veterinary reference.

Your regular veterinarian's full name:
Vet's clinic address:
Vet's clinic phone number:
How long have you been a client of this vet?
Personal references who are familiar with your experience as a pet owner and who are not members of your family or household.

Name: E-mail address:
Phone number(s):   Best time to call:
How does this person know you and your pets?

Name: E-mail address:
Phone number(s):   Best time to call:
How does this person know you and your pets?

What type of food will you feed your pet?

Who will be responsible for feeding this pet?

If your pet does something you don't like, how will you approach the problem?

Describe the pet you want to adopt:

Sex   ___No Preference ___Male ___Female

Color _____No preference ___

Age Preference: _____Baby _____Adolescent _____ Adult ____Older Adult

Size Preference:

If a particular pet seems suitable in all other ways, I would be willing to consider a different

    ___Sex ___Color ___Size ___Age

Would you consider a mixed-breed?

How did you learn about our group?

If we do not have a suitable pet for you, would you like us to refer your application to other rescue organizations?

If there is any other information you think will help us screen your application, please tell us:

SAMPLE FOSTER CARETAKER APPLICATION

Note: This is a generic sample form — you may want to add or omit questions specific to the species or breed that you rescue. A template that you can modify is available at www.rescue-matters.com.

Our Rescue Group   E-mail us at e-mail@ouraddress.com
Ourtown, U.S.A.   1-800-call-now
On the web at OurRescueGroup.com

I understand and agree that I am volunteering my time and services and will not be compensated by [name of organization]. I also understand that I may be removed from this position according to the organization's rules and procedures.

Your full name:
Your street address:
City, State, and Zip Code:
Mailing address (if different from above):
E-mail address:
How often do you check your e-mail?
Home phone:
Cell phone:
Work phone:
Preferred Phone Number: Best Time to Call:

Name and Relationship to applicant of all other adults in the home:

Name, age, sex, and relationship to applicant of all children in the home:

Do you own or rent your home?

If you rent do you have your landlord's permission to foster an animal for rescue?

Landlord's name: Landlord's phone:

How many pets are you allowed to have in your home according to your rental agreement, local ordinances, or neighborhood covenant?

Why do you want to foster a [type or breed of animal]?

Is anyone in your household allergic to [type of animal]?

Do all members of your household agree to have a foster animal in your home?

Do all household members understand and agree that each foster animal will be adopted into a new, permanent home?

How many hours a day will your foster animal spend without human companionship?

Where will your foster animal stay when you are not home?

Where will your foster animal be when you are home?

Where will your foster animal sleep at night?

Please list all pets that you own, including the following information for each one (use an addition sheet if necessary):
Type/breed of animal:
Sex: Is the animal spayed or neutered?
If not spayed or neutered, please explain why not:
Age: How long have your owned this animal?

How many pets have you owned in the past 10 years?

Please give the name, species/breed, age, sex, spay/neuter status of each pet you have owned in the past 10 years but no longer own, and what happened to each:

Have you ever fostered animals for another rescue group or shelter? Please be specific:

Are you currently fostering for another rescue group or shelter or rescue? Please be specific:

Experience With [Type of Animal]
The following questions help us assess your experience so that we can place an appropriate foster animal in your home. You do not need experience in all of these areas to be approved as a foster home. Circle all that apply, and describe your specific experience:

Basic training:
Modifying a behavior problem:
Caring for a pregnant female:
Caring for newborns:
Raising [puppies, kittens, bunnies] until ready to be placed in new homes:
Caring for an elderly animal, or one with a chronic health problem:
Socialization (exposure to other pets, strangers, children, and various experiences):
Other training [supplement with specific questions relevant to the animals]:

Are you comfortable with [animals] you do not know? Explain:

Please describe all rescue-related experience you have had:

Please describe other experiences that you feel will help you work with rescued animals:

Aside from fostering [animals], are there other ways in which you would like to help our rescue efforts? Mark all that apply and add whatever information you feel is relevant. Would you:

Talk to approved applicants about an animal you are fostering

Transport foster animals

Assist with screening adoption applications (for example, checking with personal references)

Photograph foster and potential foster animals

Evaluate an animal for rescue

Perform home checks

How long are you willing to foster an animal?

Is there any time of year during which you would typically not be able to foster an animal?

What circumstances would cause you to return a foster animal in your care?

What equipment needed for fostering do you own? [cages, crates, grooming equipment, etc.]

Do you agree to provide, at your expense, food and toys for a foster pet? (Please note: approved medical expenses are typically reimbursed by [the organization]).

How much time per day can you spend interacting with a foster animal?

Temperament and behavior problems may emerge after an animal enters foster care. Are you prepared to handle behavioral issues with assistance and guidance from the organization?

What behaviors or temperament issues would you find intolerable in a foster animal?

Foster animals are sometimes euthanized for severe behavioral or health issues. Do you understand and accept this?

References

Please provide the name and address of your current veterinarian and at least two people (not relatives) who have personal knowledge of your experience working with [type of animal].

Veterinarian's full name:
Phone:
Vet's full address:

Personal Reference 1 – full name:
Phone:
How does this person know you?

Personal Reference 2 – full name:
Phone:
How does this person know you?

Would you be willing to let one of our representatives visit your home by appointment?
If not, why?

Please provide any other information you feel would help us evaluate your application:

All of the above information I have given is true and complete. I agree to follow all the Rules and Procedures of [the organization]. I understand that I will decide whether or not to foster any particular animal. I will not hold [the organization] responsible for any damage, injury, or harm caused directly or indirectly to any person or property by any animal I may decide to foster or volunteer my time to help. [The organization] reserves the right to refuse any applicant without explanation.

Signature_____

Date_____

APPENDIX

2

Resources

Many excellent resources for rescuers exist in print and on line. In fact, a quick search will yield hundreds of sources of information on everything from general issues concerning rescue to specific types of animals to training methods and health care, and new books, articles, and web sites appear almost daily. Since this is not a reference book, I have necessarily limited the resources listed to just a few for dog and cat rescuers. Additional books and on-line sources are listed on my web site at http://www.rescuematters.com.

To find out about books, including the newest books on various subjects, search amazon.com by topic, then indicate that books should be listed by date of publication. Alpinepub.com and DogWise.com list many excellent books about dogs in their catalogs. Storey Publishing, storey.com, has books on farm animals as well as pets. The Internet is constantly changing, and new rescue organizations appear often, so the best way to find current web sites and up-to-date information on specific rescue-related topics and organizations is to search with parameters such as "rescue + breed or species (+ location or health issue or other specific topics)." The web sites listed here and at rescuematters.com will get you started.

GENERAL INTEREST FOR RESCUERS

My web site at http://www.rescuematters.com includes articles and links to other animal-related sites, including the RescueMatters discussion list, a forum for discussion of issues of concern to rescuers.

The National Animal Interest Alliance (NAIA)

The NAIA was formed to protect and promote humane practices and relationships between people and animals through education and to dispel some of the misinformation propagated by animal-rights activists. The NAIA serves as a clearinghouse for information and as an access point for subject matter experts, keynote speakers, and issue analysis. http://www.naiaonline.org

Animal-related Legislation

Rescuers should be aware of legislation that affects our right to keep animals, and informed about the implications of animal laws. The following web sites post links to and discussions about new and proposed legislation.

http://www.naiaonline.org (see above) – Of special interest is the printable brochure, A *Guide to Constructing Successful, Pet-friendly Ordinances* at http://www.naiaonline.org/pdfs/PetFriendlyGuide.pdf.

http://www. akc.org/canine_legislation/index.cfm – Much of the legislation extends to all pets, not just dogs.

Clicker Training

Although much of the information on the following two sites is directed at dog owners, some pertains specifically to other animals, and the training principles are universal.

Karen Pryor's Clickertraining.com at http://www..clickertraining.com

Clicker Solutions at http://www..clickersolutions.com

Veterinary Resources

Internet

When using the Internet for health information, always check several sources before acting on what you read, and verify the credentials of the site as well. Some people mean well but spread potentially dangerous misinformation. Many veterinarians and vet schools offer reliable on-line information, and many breed-related web sites offer information and links to more. A good place to start looking for information and links is NetVet Veterinary Resources at http://www.netvet.wustl.edu/. Other useful sites include:

American Veterinary Medical Association (AVMA) offers an array of information on health, behavior, and other issues related to all sorts of animals. http://www. avma.org

American Holistic Veterinary Medical Association (AHVMA) web site offers a directory of holistic vets and several articles of interest to rescuers interested in alternative therapies. http://www. ahvma.org

Cornell University College of Veterinary Medicine sites at offers current information on health, disease prevention, and behavior in a variety of animals. Two links are useful: http://www.vet.cornell.edu/ and http://partnersah.vet.cornell.edu/pet

Books

Merck Publishing and Merial, *The Merck/Merial Manual for Pet Health: The Complete Pet Health Resource for Your Dog, Cat, Horse or Other Pets - in Everyday Language.* Edited by Cynthia M. Kahn and Scott Line. Rathway, NJ: Merck, 2007.

Eldredge, Debra M., DVM, *Pills for Pets: The A to Z Guide to Drugs and Medications for Your Animal Companion*, New York: Citadel Press, 2003. Very useful reference for any rescuer's or owner's bookshelf.

Shojai, Amy D. *The First-Aid Companion for Dogs & and Cats.* New York: Rodale Books, 2001. Excellent, accessible resource for rescuers and owners.

Dogs

Internet

The American Kennel Club (AKC) web site provides considerable information about AKC-recognized breeds, including links to breed clubs and rescue programs. The AKC Good Friends Program and Canine Good Citizen Test program pages also offer useful materials for rescue programs for all kinds of dogs. http://www.akc.org

The United Kennel Club (UKC) web site also offers information on most AKC recognized breeds and a number of breeds not recognized by the AKC. http://www.ukcdogs.com

The Senior Dogs Project promotes the care and adoption of older dogs, and offers information and links on the web at http://www.srdogs.com

The Gray Muzzle Organization offers grants to rescue organizations to support the fostering and adoption of seniors, and lists some excellent resources on the web at http://www.greymuzzle.org/index.htm

Books

Walkowicz, Chris. *Perfect Match: A Dog Buyer's Guide.* Hobocken, NJ: Howell, 1996). Although intended as a guide to choosing a dog, this book can be useful to rescuers for assessing potential adopters' suitability for a breed or an individual dog.

Palika, Liz. *Purebred Rescue Dog Adoption: Rewards and Realities.* Hobocken, NJ: Howell, 2004. This book is meant as a guide for adopters, but has lots of useful information for rescuers as well.

McLennan, Bardi. *Rescue Me!* Freehold, NJ: Kennel Club Books, 2007. Another book meant for adopters, but full of useful information for rescuers as well.

McConnell, Patricia and Aimee Moore. *Family Friendly Dog Training - a Six Week Program for You and Your Dog.* Madison, WI: Dog's Best Friend, 2007. Excellent book for rescuers, especially foster caretakers and adopters.

Eldredge, Debra M., DVM, Liisa D. Carlson, DVM, Delbert G. Carlson, DVM, and James M. Griffin, MD. *Dog Owner's Home Veterinary Handbook*, 4th ed. Edited by Beth Adelman. Hobocken, NJ: Howell, 2007. Excellent health reference.

Cats

Internet

The Cat Fanciers Association (CFA) provides information about the breeds it recognizes, and rescue links.
http://www.cfa.org

Cat Purebred Rescue (CPR) serves Washington state and British Columbia.
http://www.catpurebredrescue.org/

Paws of Gold Feline Rescue serves the northeastern United States.
http://www.petfinder.org/shelters/NY396.html

Specialty Purebred Cat Rescue serves Wisconsin, Illinois, and Indiana.
http://www.purebredcatrescue.org

Purebred Cat Breed Rescue supports breed rescue efforts nationally.
http://www.purebredcats.org

Books

Boneham, Sheila Webster, Ph.D. *The Complete Idiot's Guide to Getting and Owning a Cat.* New York: Alpha Books, 2003. Winner of MUSE Award from the Cat Writers Association as Best Health and Care Book of 2003. Useful for rescuers and adopters, particularly chapters on health and behavior.

Moore, Arden. *The Cat Behavior Answer Book: Practical Insights & Proven Solutions for Your Feline Questions.* North Adams, MA: Storey Publishing, 2007. More about why cats do the things that land them in rescue, and how to address those behaviors.

Eldredge, Debra M., DVM, Liisa D. Carlson, DVM, Delbert G. Carlson, DVM, and James M. Griffin, MD. *Cat Owner's Home Veterinary Handbook*, 3rd ed. Edited by Beth Adelman. Hobocken, NJ: Howell, 2007. Excellent health reference.

About the Author

Award-winning writer Sheila W. Boneham, Ph.D., has been touched by some form of animal rescue all her life. She grew up surrounded by dogs, cats, horses, and more–Chihuahuas, a Scottish Deerhound, a rescued Irish Wolfhound, two Miniature Schnauzers (Sheila found one of them coated with ice in a parking lot on a January night), a number of canine and feline mixed breeds, and two stray hamsters. She was Indiana State Equitation Champion for three years, and several of her family's equine members would now be called rescues, as would the long line of animals her family took in and rehomed.

In the early 1990's, Sheila founded and worked with rescue programs for Labrador Retrievers and Australian Shepherds, and she has served as a volunteer for several rescue organizations and shelters, teaching in-service workshops on basic dog handling techniques and breed identification as well as public courses in basic dog care, obedience, and bite prevention. Sheila has bred highly successful Australian Shepherds and has trained and titled Aussies and Labs in several canine sports.

Sheila holds a doctorate in folklore from Indiana University and taught for some 20 years at universities in Maryland, Washington, D.C., Indiana, Kuwait, and Tunisia (and yes, she brought a dog home from one of her overseas jaunts). Several of her books have been named best in their categories by the Dog Writers Association of America and the Cat Writers Association, including *Breed Rescue* (Alpine, 1998), the first book devoted to starting and running a canine rescue program.

Sheila lives in Indiana with her husband Roger, Australian Shepherd Jay, Labrador Retriever Lily, and the ever-present spirits of her other animal friends. When she isn't writing or playing with her dogs, Sheila paints, gardens, and teaches writing and creativity classes. You can reach her and her RescueMatters discussion list through her websites at www.sheilaboneham.com and www.rescuematters.com.

INDEX